CHRISTLike
Supernatural

Juan J. Vasquez

Cover design by Juan J. Vasquez

Cover picture, "Healing of the Blind Man," by Brian Jekel

ISBN-13: 978-0-9991254-0-3

ISBN E-book: 978-0-9991254-1-0

Printed in the U.S.A.

Acknowledgments

I would first like to thank God for giving me the grace to finish this book. Everything I have accomplished has been because of Him. He has preserved, saved, and healed me. All the glory belongs to Jesus. Second, I want to thank my wife for all of her support and encouragement during the process of writing this book. Ana K., my love, many people do not get to see what you do behind the curtains, but I certainly do. You are amazing and I would not change you for anyone else in the world. I want to thank my father, Juan Vasquez, my mother, Carmen Bello (without you I wouldn't even be alive today), my grandmother, Isabel Espinosa, and my stepfather, Alexis W. Mendoza, for every sacrifice you made in raising me. Finally, I would like to thank my blood and church family. You have believed in me and have been with me through the whole process of writing this book. Although this book was professionally edited by FirstEditing.com, I would like to give a special thanks to my friends and family for reading, commenting, and helping me to edit the English and Spanish versions of this book. I love you guys.

Dedication

I dedicate this book to the kingdom of God and the universal church of the Lord Jesus Christ. I pray that you would be built up and equipped to fulfill the Great Commission with power and love.

Table of Contents

Preface vii

"Follow Me and I Will Make You Fishers of Men" 1

Jesus 5

The Twelve 9

The Early Church and Beyond 15

Precautions 21

Be Filled With the Holy Spirit 27

Just Believe 33

Hearing the Voice of God 39

The Gifts of the Holy Spirit 43

Healing and Evangelism Part 1 47

Healing and Evangelism Part 2 55

Deliverance and Evangelism Part 1 63

Deliverance and Evangelism Part 2 69

Words of Knowledge and Evangelism 79

Discernment of Spirits and Evangelism 87

Prophecy and Evangelism 93

Miracles and Evangelism 103

Tongues and Evangelism 111

Dreams, Visions and Evangelism 119

Cooperating with Angels in Evangelism 127

The Gospel and Evangelism 137

Anointed Preaching and Evangelism 143

Prayer and Evangelism 149

Revival and Evangelism 157

Conclusion 171

Appendix: Treasure Hunt 175

Bibliography 179

Recommended Material 181

Preface

I am going to be completely honest with you. I have an agenda as I write this book. My goals are:

1. To *convince* you that the most effective[1] way of evangelizing the lost is through preaching the gospel and operating in the gifts and power of the Holy Spirit.
2. To *motivate* you to focus your greatest efforts towards winning the lost through this type of evangelism.

I believe that power evangelism[2]—preaching the gospel together with a demonstration of the power and gifts of the Holy Spirit—*is* New Testament evangelism. I believe power evangelism *is* the form of evangelism Jesus practiced, taught His disciples, and was practiced by the early church.

It is my conviction that everything else we do should work as a complement to power evangelism. We should feed the poor, clothe the naked, visit those in prison, and perform social justice. But when we substitute, instead of complementing, power evangelism for these good but man-made efforts, we end up fishing for men with lines when we could be doing so with nets.

---

[1] By "effective," I mean it is the way to win the most souls with the least amount of human effort and engineering, which creates the most com-mitted and firm disciples.

[2] This phrase, "power evangelism," is not my own. I first heard this term from John Wimber, one of the founding members of the Vineyard movement.

Lives are at risk. Time is running out. Millions are perishing. It's time we get the job done with the tools and instructions given to us by God. New Testament evangelism is power evangelism and power evangelism was Jesus' way of evangelism.

So if we want to follow in His footsteps, if we want to be *Christ-like* in our way of evangelizing, then our evangelism must be *Supernatural*.

"Follow Me and I Will Make You Fishers of Men"

¹⁰ ... And Jesus said to Simon, "Do not fear, from now on you will be catching men." ¹¹ When they had brought their boats to land, they left everything and followed Him. (Luke 5:10-11)

This story in Luke 5:1-11 serves as a great illustration to the effectiveness of evangelizing as Jesus did. In this portion, Luke tells us that Jesus came down to a lake in Galilee. He was teaching a group of people, most likely about the kingdom of God. It seems that as He was teaching, the group became a multitude and in order to continue teaching, He got into the closest boat, which belonged to some fishermen. The water provided some distance between Him and the growing population and it also provided great acoustics for the people to hear Him better.

As His message came to an end, He turned and told one of the fishermen, named Simon Peter, to head out into deep water. Jesus wanted to take him and his companions on a fishing trip. The only problem, according to Peter who was a business man and a professional at catching fish, was that there were no fish at that time of the day. Matter of fact, Peter and his buddies had been fishing all night and couldn't catch anything!

But it seems that out of respect to this Rabbi, Peter did what he was told. He went out into deep water and cast the nets. Unexpectedly, the water began to bubble, and the nets began to fill! Peter and his crew rushed to bring in the

1

fish, but the catch was so big that the nets were tearing and he called over his partners, the Zebedee's, for help. Even with two boats and various fishermen, the catch of fish was so large their boats almost sank.

When Peter realized what happened, fear gripped his heart and he fell in reverence before this holy man of God. He then confessed his sinfulness. But instead of being rejected and condemned, Jesus made Peter and his associates a proposition: "Follow me, and I will make you fishers of men" (Matthew 4:19).

Now, if we look no further, this story seems to be nothing more than an account of how Jesus called a group of fishermen. But I believe it is also an illustration of how Jesus evangelized. There are actually a few lessons that we can learn from this account.

1. Our way of catching "fish" is not as effective as Jesus'

Although Peter was a successful and professional fisherman, when this carpenter turned Rabbi came around, things changed. Under the most unlikely circumstances, Peter caught more fish in one day than he probably had caught in one year!

I'm not advocating for us to give up all efforts that involve human ingenuity and effort, but I am looking towards a future where we do not minor on the majors, and do not major on the minors. Let's be honest, where have all our programs, concerts, and services left us? It's left us with a church that is stagnating, decreasing, and becoming increasingly secular, especially in the West.

2. Jesus' way of catching "fish" is supernatural

How did so many fish gather at the right place, at the right time? Peter and his crew had been out there all night! Either they were miraculously drawn there by God, or Jesus had a word of knowledge of where they were. Either way, the catch was supernatural!

As we are going to see in the following chapters, people have been brought to salvation through supernatural encounters time and time again. There is nothing natural about the gospel. This gospel must be proclaimed and demonstrated supernaturally. Any presentation of the gospel without the supernatural is less than what God intended.

3. The harvest that will come from following Jesus' example will be so abundant that we will need more laborers

I imagine Peter and his coworkers throwing their nets over and over the night before Jesus arrived at their shore. But when Jesus stepped on board and they obeyed His instructions, they witnessed a miracle – a catch of fish more numerous than they could handle at once!

This form of evangelism will bring in such a harvest of souls that we will need the cooperation of the body of Christ, working together as a whole, to disciple these people.

What Jesus did with these fishermen that day was intended to be a lesson to them. It was even implied in His invitation, "Guys you haven't seen anything yet. Follow me, observe my ways, imitate my example, and you will "catch" as many men as you have fish with me on this day" (my paraphrase).

My brethren, I plead with you. Let us follow Jesus' example. The harvest is plentiful, the harvest is ripe. God just needs laborers who are willing and know how to follow His lead. Let us be like Christ in our evangelism. His way of "fishing men" is much more effective, abundant, and long-lasting. Let the words of Jesus echo in your spirit, "Follow me and I will make you fishers of men."

Jesus

You know of Jesus of Nazareth, how God anointed Him with the Holy Spirit and with power, and how He went about doing good and healing all who were oppressed by the devil, for God was with Him. (Acts 10:38)

There is no mention of Jesus doing anything miraculous before He began His public ministry at the age of thirty. But as soon as He was baptized in water by John the Baptist, the Holy Spirit came upon Him, an audible voice from heaven affirmed His Son-ship and He was led into the wilderness by the Spirit where He confronted and overcame several temptations from Satan (Matthew 4:1-11; Mark 1:9-13; Luke 4:1-13).

Immediately after this, Luke records that, "Jesus returned to Galilee in the power of the Spirit..." (4:14). He then entered a synagogue where He read a prophecy that would define and summarize the work He was there to do:

[17] And the book of the prophet Isaiah was handed to Him. And He opened the book and found the place where it was written,

[18] 'THE SPIRIT OF THE LORD IS UPON ME,
BECAUSE HE ANOINTED ME TO PREACH THE
GOSPEL TO THE POOR.
HE HAS SENT ME TO PROCLAIM RELEASE TO
THE CAPTIVES,
AND RECOVERY OF SIGHT TO THE BLIND,
TO SET FREE THOSE WHO ARE OPPRESSED,

¹⁹ TO PROCLAIM THE FAVORABLE YEAR OF
THE LORD.'

Here is what Isaiah was prophesying about Jesus.
First, that He would be anointed and have power because
the Holy Spirit would be upon Him (v18a). Second, that
Jesus would proclaim a message of salvation and freedom
to the people (v18b-c, 19). Third, that Jesus would physically heal the sick (v18d). Lastly, that Jesus would deliver
the oppressed (v18e).

In other words, the ministry of Jesus would involve
power, proclamation, healing, and deliverance. This is exactly what we see over and over again throughout the ministry of Jesus. "And He went into their synagogues throughout all Galilee, preaching and casting out the demons"
(Mark 1:39).

> ²³ Jesus was going throughout all Galilee,
> teaching in their synagogues and proclaiming
> the gospel of the kingdom, and healing every
> kind of disease and every kind of sickness
> among the people. ²⁴ The news about Him
> spread throughout all Syria; and they brought
> to Him all who were ill, those suffering with
> various diseases and pains, demoniacs, epi-
> leptics, paralytics; and He healed them.
> ²⁵ Large crowds followed Him from Galilee
> and *the* Decapolis and Jerusalem and Judea
> and *from* beyond the Jordan (Matthew 4:23-
> 25).

Whether Jesus was in a social gathering, such as the
wedding at Cana (John 2:1-12), staying at the home of a
friend (Matthew 8:14-17), or traveling from place to place

(Matthew 14:22-36), the supernatural wasn't too far behind. Everywhere He went, Jesus taught and proclaimed the Kingdom, but He also demonstrated its reality by healing the sick, delivering the oppressed, and performing miraculous signs.

This duo of proclamation with demonstration brought multitudes to hear Jesus, seek Jesus, and believe in Jesus. Jesus was the ultimate fisher of men. He evangelized with power. His evangelism was supernatural and the people knew it.

> [22] They were amazed at His teaching; for He was teaching them as *one* having authority, and not as the scribes... [27] They were all amazed, so that they debated among themselves, saying, "What is this? A new teaching with authority! He commands even the unclean spirits, and they obey Him." [28] Immediately the news about Him spread every-where into all the surrounding district of Galilee (Mark 1:22, 27-28).

The people had been accustomed to the dry and powerless teachings of the Pharisees. But then Jesus came and demonstrated that the God who parted the Red Sea and guided the Israelites in the wilderness with the cloud and fire was still active and present in their day.

In like manner, people today are hungering for something real. They've seen a form of godliness without any power. What they need is a church operating in the supernatural just like its founder Jesus Christ. I am not talking about emotionalism, hype, and fluff. I am talking about power evangelism – preaching the gospel with signs following.

From beginning to end, this was how Jesus operated. This was how He evangelized. Each step of His journey and ministry, from Galilee to Jerusalem, was filled with power evangelism. Even at the time of His arrest, Jesus healed the ear of one of His persecutors (Luke 22:51).

We must follow in His footsteps. He will teach us how to fish for men. His way is supernatural and it is the most effective. Will you rise to the challenge?

The Twelve

Everyone kept feeling a sense of awe; and many wonders and signs were taking place through the apostles. (Acts 2:43)

After beginning His public ministry, Jesus began to gather a large following. People were drawn to Him because of His compassion for the sick and His friendliness to sinners. His teaching was new, radical, and with authority. This man was fearless. In addition to this, the supernatural accompanied His teaching and preaching everywhere He went. He was on a mission and nothing could stop Him.

But He needed help. The harvest was plentiful and the laborers were few. On top of that, after completing His goal and returning to where He came from, who would continue the work? Jesus decided to choose twelve men—twelve, just like the tribes of Israel.

> [12] It was at this time that He went off to the mountain to pray, and He spent the whole night in prayer to God. [13] And when day came, He called His disciples to Him and chose twelve of them, whom He also named as apostles: [14] Simon, whom He also named Peter, and Andrew his brother; and James and John; and Philip and Bartholomew; [15] and Matthew and Thomas; James *the son* of Alphaeus, and Simon who was called the Zealot; [16] Judas *the son* of James, and Judas

Iscariot, who became a traitor. (Luke 6:12-16)

These were the men who would continue His work and His mission in His way. These were the men He would train and teach to believe and do what He did. They would build and expand His kingdom.

Now what did the disciples see Jesus do after He chose them? What did they experience as they stayed with Him night after night? We do not have to look hard. According to Luke's account, in the very next verse we see,

> [17] Jesus came down with them and stood on a level place; and *there was* a large crowd of His disciples, and a great throng of people from all Judea and Jerusalem and the coastal region of Tyre and Sidon, [18] who had come to hear Him and to be healed of their diseases; and those who were troubled with unclean spirits were being cured. [19] And all the people were trying to touch Him, for power was coming from Him and healing *them* all. (Luke 6:17-19)

Their first lesson on how to continue the work of Christ, on how to fish for men was:

1. Teach the people
2. Heal the people
3. Deliver the people

The people came to hear Jesus (v18). The rest of Chapter 6 is dedicated to what He actually taught them. People hunger to hear the unadulterated word of God. God's word brings hope (Jeremiah 29:11), increases faith (Romans

10:17), provides guidance and direction (Psalm 119:105), is able to teach, rebuke, correct, and train us in righteousness (2 Timothy 3:16-17), and it makes us wise for salvation (2 Timothy 3:15).

Jesus preached and taught the gospel of the kingdom because it alone is able to save us (Romans 1:16). But notice He also demonstrated and confirmed it with the supernatural (Luke 6:18-19).

If we go further in the Gospel of Luke, we can see that the disciples continue to see Jesus repeating this pattern. In 7:1-10, He healed a centurion's servant with His words. In 7:11-17 He raised a widow's son from the dead. In 7:18-23, Jesus points to His supernatural works as a demonstration of His mission and identity. In 8:1, He travels from village to village proclaiming and preaching the kingdom of God. In 8:22-25, the disciples witness Jesus exercising His authority over nature. In 8:26-39, Jesus delivers a man possessed by a legion of demons. In 8:40-56, He heals a woman and raises a little girl from the dead.

Then we come around to Chapter 9, where Jesus now expects His followers to put into practice what He has shown them. Here is how they were to evangelize, fish for men, and establish and expand the kingdom of God:

> And He called the twelve together, and gave them power and authority over all the demons and to heal diseases. ² And He sent them out to proclaim the kingdom of God and to perform healing (9:1-2)... ⁷And as you go, preach, saying, 'The kingdom of heaven is at hand.' ⁸Heal *the* sick, raise *the* dead, cleanse

the lepers, cast out demons. Freely you received, freely give (Matthew 10:7-8).

When the disciples returned from their short mission's trip, they reported to Him everything that happened (9:10). Then He went back into His normal routine of preaching the kingdom and healing the sick (9:11).

Can you see the pattern? Can you see what evangelism was to Jesus? It was proclamation coupled with demonstration. This is what He taught His followers to do. Jesus' way of evangelism was power evangelism. And power evangelism is New Testament evangelism.

Even before Jesus left this earth, He reminded His disciples,

> [15] … Go into all the world and preach the gospel to all creation. [16] He who has believed and has been baptized shall be saved; but he who has disbelieved shall be condemned. [17] These signs will accompany those who have believed: in My name they will cast out demons, they will speak with new tongues; [18] they will pick up serpents, and if they drink any deadly poison, it will not hurt them; they will lay hands on the sick, and they will recover.

> [19] So then, when the Lord Jesus had spoken to them, He was received up into heaven and sat down at the right hand of God. [20] And they went out and preached everywhere, while the Lord worked with them, and confirmed the word by the signs that followed. (Mark 16:15-20)

When Jesus left and ascended into heaven, the disciples continued His work in the same fashion. In Acts 2, they were supernaturally filled with the Holy Spirit and Peter proclaimed the word of God. As a result, three thou-sand people were saved (2:41). In Acts 3, Peter and John healed a paralyzed man and then preached. By the end of the day, about five thousand men were saved (4:4).

I could go on, but I think you get the point. The supernatural + the preaching of the gospel = power evangelism, which results in a great harvest of souls.

This is how Jesus evangelized. This is how He won the lost. This is what He taught His disciples. So is this what you are doing today?

The Early Church and Beyond

For the promise is for you and your children and for all who are far off, as many as the Lord our God will call to Himself. (Acts 2:39)

One of the biggest objections of cessationists[3] towards the continuation of the supernatural as a normal part of the life of the church is that they believe it was only intended to validate or confirm the apostles and their preaching of the gospel until the Bible was completed. But there is a problem with this line of argumentation – the apostles of Christ were not the only ones who moved in the supernatural and evangelized the lost with power.

After the successful mission of the twelve apostles, Jesus decided to send out 70 disciples more to continue the work He had started.

> [1]Now after this the Lord appointed seventy others, and sent them in pairs ahead of Him to every city and place where He Himself was going to come... [8] Whatever city you enter and they receive you, eat what is set before you; [9] and heal those in it who are sick, and say to them, 'The kingdom of God has come near to you.'(Luke 10:1, 8-9)

---

[3] Those who believe that the regular practice and manifestations of the gifts of the Holy Spirit "ceased" in the first century after the writing of the last book of the Bible.

And when they had returned from their own evangelistic efforts,

> [17] The seventy returned with joy, saying, "Lord, even the demons are subject to us in Your name." [18] And He said to them, "I was watching Satan fall from heaven like lightning. [19] Behold, I have given you authority to tread on serpents and scorpions, and over all the power of the enemy, and nothing will injure you. [20] Nevertheless do not rejoice in this, that the spirits are subject to you, but rejoice that your names are recorded in heaven." (Luke 10:17-20)

So here is this group of nameless believers who go out to evangelize and are given the same instructions as the twelve apostles. They were to proclaim the kingdom and heal the sick. When they returned, they even reported casting out spirits (v17).

If we continue into the book of Acts, we notice that after choosing the first deacons of the church, a man named Stephen was doing the same thing Jesus and the twelve apostles did while he served at the tables! "[7] The word of God kept on spreading; and the number of the disciples continued to increase greatly in Jerusalem, and a great many of the priests were becoming obedient to the faith. [8] And Stephen, full of grace and power, was performing great wonders and signs among the people" (Acts 6:7-8).

Two chapters later another deacon, Philip, decides to go evangelize as he flees persecution and the same pattern is seen in his ministry.

⁴ Therefore, those who had been scattered went about preaching the word. ⁵ Philip went down to the city of Samaria and *began* proclaiming Christ to them. ⁶ The crowds with one accord were giving attention to what was said by Philip, as they heard and saw the signs which he was performing. ⁷ For *in the case of* many who had unclean spirits, they were coming out *of them* shouting with a loud voice; and many who had been paralyzed and lame were healed. ⁸ So there was much rejoicing in that city. (Acts 8:4-8)

So here is what we can conclude about what we have seen in the Scriptures. Power evangelism is the New Testament form of evangelism. Jesus, the apostles, and the early church evangelized by preaching the gospel and demonstrating it with signs following.

In many Bibles, the book of Acts is titled, "The Acts of the Apostles." But as many have said before me, a better title to suit this book is "The Acts of the Holy Ghost." As long as the Holy Spirit is present within the Church and every believer, the supernatural is sure to follow.

Here is the simple truth, these "acts" were not limited to Jesus, His disciples, or even to the early church of the first century. We can do them also. Not only can we do them, we should do them.

Jesus said: "Truly, truly, I say to you, he who believes in Me, the works that I do, he will do also; and greater *works* than these he will do; because I go to the Father." (John 14:12)

> [17] "These signs will accompany those who have believed: in My name they will cast out demons, they will speak with new tongues; [18] they will pick up serpents, and if they drink any deadly *poison*, it will not hurt them; they will lay hands on the sick, and they will recover." (Mark 16:17-18)

The Bible even lets us know that if someone is sick, they should be able to come to the church and receive healing.

> [14] "Is anyone among you sick? *Then* he must call for the elders of the church and they are to pray over him, anointing him with oil in the name of the Lord; [15] and the prayer offered in faith will restore the one who is sick, and the Lord will raise him up, and if he has committed sins, they will be forgiven him. [16] Therefore, confess your sins to one another, and pray for one another so that you may be healed. The effective prayer of a righteous man can accomplish much." (James 5:14-16)

There is no expiration date stamped on any of these promises. Nowhere is it stated that the supernatural would occur depending on what era you lived in or what ministry position you held. The supernatural was so natural to the early church. So what happened? We could mention many reasons. But one things is for sure, the idea that God no longer works that way or requires us to do so is not Biblical.

"For all the promises of God in Him *are* Yes, and in Him Amen, to the glory of God through us" (2 Corinthians 1:20). "There is no favoritism with God" (Romans 2:11

NIV). "Jesus Christ *is* the same yesterday and today and forever" (Hebrews 13:8).

Let me tell you—if He did it before, He can do it again. And He is doing it. Will you let Him do it through you?

Precautions

15 Some, to be sure, are preaching Christ even from envy and strife, but some also from good will; 16 the latter do it out of love… 17 the former proclaim Christ out of selfish ambition rather than from pure motives (Philippians 1:15-17)

Before we step into the how-to's of power evangelism, I believe a word of caution is in order. Our motivations and perspectives will determine whether we flourish or fail in our endeavor to share the gospel super-naturally. So let's get our ducks in a row before we proceed any further.

Our motivation

We all need to answer the question of why. Why do we evangelize? Why do we go on missions trips? Why do we share the gospel? Why should we move in the supernatural? A ship may have its course planned out, but if its rudder is broken or slanted in the wrong direction, it will end up somewhere else.

I have seen a lot of people get involved in ministry, service in the community, or evangelism for right and wrong reasons. Whatever is in a person's heart will eventually come out into the light, "for out of the abundance of the heart the mouth speaks" (Matthew 12:34). And sometimes what comes out has the ability to affect not only oneself, but also those who are around for better or for worse.

I propose that our greatest motivations for why we do anything in life is God's glory and love for people. Paul said, "Whatever you do in word or deed, *do* all in the name of the Lord Jesus, giving thanks through Him to God the Father" (Colossians 3:17). Jesus said, "Let your light shine before men in such a way that they may see your good works, and glorify your Father who is in heaven" (Matthew 5:16). Our first and primary reason for learning to operate in the supernatural for evangelism is that God may be glorified. It is not to make a name for ourselves, build a kingdom for ourselves, or gain financial profit for our-selves. We do what we do so that God may shine and receive all the glory.

But close to the heart of God are people. The greatest way to honor Him is to love one another. The Bible says,

> If I speak with the tongues of men and of angels, but do not have love, I have become a noisy gong or a clanging cymbal. ² If I have *the gift of* prophecy, and know all mysteries and all knowledge; and if I have all faith, so as to remove mountains, but do not have love, I am nothing. ³ And if I give all my possessions to feed *the poor*, and if I sur-render my body to be burned, but do not have love, it profits me nothing. (1 Corinthians 13:1-3)

We must understand that "knowledge puffs up, but love builds up" (1 Corinthians 8:1). So we should learn all we can but for the purpose of loving people and building others up.

Fruits vs. Gifts

There is a dilemma I have noticed in Pentecostal and Charismatic circles. Many view those with strong spiritual abilities as being more spiritual and mature than those who don't have them. If a person speaks in tongues, prophecies and casts out spirits they are seen as being elite Christians. But allow me to burst some bubbles here.

Gifts do not determine spiritual maturity; fruits do. See, gifts are exactly that – gifts. They are special graces given to people by God that has no basis on personal merit. But a person's fruits is a testament to their character. The gifts are evidence that the Holy Spirit is upon you, while the fruit is evidence that He lives in you. Gifts demonstrate you have power, while fruits demonstrate that you are saved.

> [21] "Not everyone who says to Me, 'Lord, Lord,' will enter the kingdom of heaven, but he who does the will of My Father who is in heaven *will enter*. [22] Many will say to Me on that day, 'Lord, Lord, did we not prophesy in Your name, and in Your name cast out demons, and in Your name perform many miracles?' [23] And then I will declare to them, 'I never knew you; depart from Me, you who practice lawlessness.'" (Matthew 7:21-23)

Can I tell you something? I have seen many people crash and burn because they had this mixed up. They rose up in Christian stardom, but because of a lack of character, they did not remain. Our gifts open doors for us, but it is our fruit that will keep them open.

We need both the fruit and the gifts of the Holy Spirit. To be lacking in either area is to be an incomplete reflection of Jesus.

The Kingdom

The idea that power evangelism is New Testament evangelism might cause some to wonder, "What then of all the other types of kingdom work? Are they not valid expressions of evangelism?" Yes, they are valid, but incomeplete.

If you look at the New Testament, what can be seen is that power evangelism is to be a part of every effort to reach the lost. You can feed the hungry and minister supernaturally to people's needs. Look at Jesus and the deacons who did so themselves. You can be next to some-one on the grocery line or at a bus stop and have a prophetic word for them (see John 4 for the story of Jesus and the Samaritan woman). You can visit a friend's home and heal a family member of a fever (see Matthew 8:14-15). You can be on your way to church and minister to someone along the way (see Acts 3:1-10).

Can you imagine being at war and receiving words of knowledge about your enemy's strategies? (see 2 Kings 6). Can you imagine interpreting a dream your boss or even a great leader of a nation might have (i.e., Joseph and Daniel)? There are no limits in how we can serve God.

But the supernatural was meant to be an ordinary factor of every Christian's life. You can evangelize like this in any context. Not everyone may need physical healing; but they may need emotional healing, spiritual healing (deliverance), or even a prophetic word. We should not become discouraged of doing any other forms of kingdom work, but it should be united with the supernatural.

Let Scripture be your Guide

There are many who limit what God can do because they base their ideas and opinions on past experiences, the failures of others, or denominational traditions. As Christians, we live by conviction, not by emotions, traditions, or past experiences. We operate out of what the Bible says. If the Bible says it, I will believe it; I will obey it.

On the flip side of this, also make sure to test everything in light of scripture. The Bible says, "test the spirits" (1 John 4:1) and "[21]examine everything *carefully*; hold fast to that which is good; [22] abstain from every form of evil" (1 Thessalonians 5:21-22). So whatever visions, dreams, or prophetic words you give or receive, make sure it aligns with the word and will of God.

With these precautions in place, let's proceed with the purpose that has been placed before us.

Be Filled With the Holy Spirit

And do not get drunk with wine, for that is dissipation, but be filled with the Spirit. (Ephesians 5:18)

There is no way around it—if you want operate in the supernatural, you must be filled with the Holy Spirit. There is much debate around this topic, concerning questions such as "What is it? When does it happen? Is it still for today? What is the evidence it has taken place?" I will give you my perspective.

Terminology

If you read the following passages (Matthew 3:11; Mark 1:8; Luke 3:16; John 1:26, 33; Acts 1:5; 11:16; 2:4; 4:31; 9:17; 13:9, 52; Ephesians 4:31; Acts 19:2; Galatians 3:2), you will notice that the phrases, "baptism of/with the Holy Spirit," "filled with the Holy Spirit," and "receiving the Spirit," are used interchangeably in the New Testament to describe the same experience.

What is it?

The baptism of the Holy Spirit is the experience of having the third person of the Trinity come upon a believer to overwhelm them with or submerge them into His power. This experience is different to being indwelt (John 14:17; 1 Corinthians 6:19; Romans 8:11) or sealed (Ephesians 1:13; 4:30) by the Holy Spirit. When this happens, the believer receives supernatural power, strength, might and ability (Acts 1:8).

This was something that was promised by God in the book of Joel (2:28-29), prophesied by John the Baptist in the gospels (Matthew 3:11; Mark 1:8; Luke 3:16; John 1:26, 33) and commanded by Jesus before His departure from this earth (Acts 1:4-5).

When Does it Occur?

Although there are examples of people being baptized in the Spirit at the time of their conversion (see Acts 10 with the household of Cornelius), this normally takes place subsequent to salvation. For example, the twelve disciples and some other believers were baptized with the Spirit in Acts 2, even though they had received the Spirit prior to Jesus' ascension into heaven (John 20:22). They even experienced being filled again after a time of prayer in Acts 4:31.

Another example is when Philip went into Samaria and preached the gospel (Acts 8:5). Many people got saved and were even baptized (8:12-13), but it was not until the apostles Peter and John laid their hands on them that they received this blessing (8:14-17).

In Acts 9, after his encounter with Jesus Christ, Paul was prayed for by a man named Ananias. It was at that moment that he was filled (v17-19). In Acts 19, Paul then ministers in a city called Ephesus and finds a group of people who had been baptized by John in water. After talking with them, Paul baptizes them in water again and lays his hands on them to receive the Holy Spirit. "⁶ And when Paul had laid his hands upon them, the Holy Spirit came on them, and they *began* speaking with tongues and prophesying" (v6).

From these passages, we understand that a person can experience this filling at the time of their conversion (Acts 10) or after their conversion (Acts 2, 8, 9, and 19). Even better, this is not a one-time event (Acts 4:31). We are to continually be filled with the Holy Spirit (Ephesians 5:18).

Why do we need it?

There are many ways to answer this question. But it boils down to this. We cannot be effective witnesses without it. Jesus said, "but you will receive power when the Holy Spirit has come upon you; and you shall be My witnesses both in Jerusalem, and in all Judea and Samaria, and even to the remotest part of the earth" (Acts 1:8). First we need His power, then we can be His witnesses.

Did you know that chronologically, the last words Jesus told His disciples, before He ascended into heaven, was not "Go?" It was "Wait." They were to stay in Jerusalem and wait for the promise of the Holy Spirit (Acts 1:4). Just think about that; if Jesus needed this power to be effective in His ministry (Luke 3:21-22; 4:18-19), what makes us think that we can do more with less?

How can we know we have received it?

The traditional Pentecostal view says that speaking in tongues is the initial evidence of a person being baptized in the Spirit. They point to what happened in Acts 2, 10, and 19 as support. My only problem with this view is that it is too narrow. Out of eight references where a person or a group of people were described as being filled with the Spirit, tongues is only clearly mentioned in three chapters.

I believe the greatest evidence that someone has been filled with the Spirit is if one or more supernatural gifts or signs manifest in a person's life.[4] Paul says,

> [7] But to each one is given the ***manifestation*** of the Spirit for the common good. [8] For to one is given the word of wisdom through the Spirit, and to another the word of knowledge according to the same Spirit; [9] to another faith by the same Spirit, and to another gifts of healing by the one Spirit, [10] and to another the effecting of miracles, and to another prophecy, and to another the distinguishing of spirits, to another *various* kinds of tongues, and to another the interpretation of tongues. (1 Corinthians 12:7-10 – emphasis mine)

Joel's prophecy says that when God's Spirit is poured out, men and women, young and old would have visions, dreams, and even prophesy. In almost every instance where the Spirit came upon an individual, supernatural phenomenon occurred (Acts 2:1-4, 17-18; 4:29-31; 6:3, 5; 8:14-18; 9:17-19; 10:44-46; 19:1-7).

---

[4] I believe that the power of the Holy Spirit includes divine authority and influence to convict and convert souls (Acts 2:37). In my opinion, this is the side of the power of the Holy Spirit that cessationists are okay with. The problem is the definition is too narrow. This power also includes the ability to heal and cast out demons just as Jesus did. So if I put it all together, I would say that when the Holy Spirit comes upon us, He gives us divine authority and influence to convict and convert souls and the ability to heal the sick, cast out demons, and operate in spiritual gifts or supernatural signs. I also do believe the baptism in the Spirit will produce supernatural boldness to preach the gospel (Acts 4:31) and supernatural strength to overcome the flesh (Ephesians 5:18; Galatians 5:16). But these would be secondary evidences.

So if we want to know if we have been filled or baptized with the Holy Spirit, then we must ask ourselves these questions: (1) Have I received power? (2) Are any of the gifts of the Spirit manifesting in my life? (3) Do I feel a desire to preach the gospel and to do it with boldness?

How can we receive it?

Before answering this question, it is important we understand that this is a gift, which means it is something we receive by grace. It cannot be earned but is freely given to us if we are believers (Acts 2:38; Galatians 3:2).

Now, there are two ways of receiving this baptism, this gift, or this filling: (1) By prayer—we must ask with faith (Luke 11:9-13; Acts 1:4, 14; 2:1-4) or (2) By impartation[5]—hands can be laid on us by someone who is filled with the Spirit (Acts 8:14-17; 9:17-18; 19:6).

It is God's will that you be filled. Without this baptism, we will not be able to do what Jesus did. And Jesus will not send you to do something without having the tools necessary to get the job done. You don't have to beg Him; you don't have to work for it. Just believe in faith. Just receive by grace. Are you ready? Here it comes!

---

[5] Transferring of anointing

Just Believe

²² And Jesus answered saying to them, "Have faith in God." (Mark 11:22)

In addition to being filled with the Spirit, if we want to see the supernatural manifest in our lives as we preach the gospel, there are two very important topics that we need to understand. The first is faith. The second is discerning the voice of God. Let's begin with the former.

The Bible teaches that faith is one of the highest virtues a person can possess (1 Corinthians 13:13). It is through faith that we are saved (Ephesians 2:8). It is by faith we move mountains (Mark 11:23-24). Our faith even acts as a shield and protects us from the darts of the enemy (Ephesians 6:17). And without faith it is impossible to please God (Hebrews 11:6).

Now, we must learn how faith works in terms of seeing the supernatural. We need faith to receive answers to prayer (James 1:6-7), operate in spiritual gifts (Romans 12:3-8; 1 Corinthians 12:7-11) and see miracles, healings, and deliverances (James 5:15; Mark 16:17-18). The great news is, that similar to salvation, faith makes the supernatural accessible to anyone who is a believer in Jesus Christ (John 14:12). In this there is no discrimination or favoritism with God (James 1:17). Since every believer has been blessed with "every spiritual blessing in heavenly places" (Ephesians 1:3), the difference between those who see the supernatural and those who don't is faith.

So What is Faith?

The Bible defines faith as, "the assurance of *things* hoped for, the conviction of things not seen" (Hebrews 11:1). The actual Greek word is *"pistis,"* which means to believe, to have confidence, to be faithful, or to be persuaded.[6] In other words, faith means to believe, have conviction of, be sure about, and be fully persuaded that God *is* who He says He is and that He will *do* what He says He will do. If you truly believe, then your actions should be in accordance with your faith (James 2:14, 17).

The Gift of Faith vs. the Fruit of Faith

In 1 Corinthians 12, Paul speaks about the gift of faith. This is not the type of faith that comes by natural means as we will see in a moment. This faith, this trust, is a spontaneous burst or empowerment from the Spirit of God to believe God for something supernatural, miraculous or humanly impossible. Steven Brooks in his book, *How to Operate in the Gifts of the Spirit*, says this about the gift of faith,

> The gift of faith takes people beyond their normal ability to believe. It is best viewed as a special or extraordinary faith that comes upon you as the Holy Spirit desires. I refer to it as 'super faith' because when it is in manifestation you feel tremendous boldness, and there is not a speck of doubt that can touch you while you are under the anointing of super faith. This is not ordinary or common

---

faith that we operate with on a day-to-day basis.[7]

When this gift of faith is in operation, nothing seems impossible. Even doubt evaporates in the heat of the Holy Spirit's power. When this faith comes upon you, do not resist it; do not doubt it. It is an indication that God is about to do something miraculous for whatever need is present.

Besides this gift of faith being at our disposal, Galatians 5 also speaks about the fruit of faith. This is the faith Paul is referring to in Romans 12:3 when he says, "God has allotted to each a measure of faith." We all have a level of faith that we operate in from day to day. This faith we possess can be increased, strengthened, and stretched just like a muscle. Charles Stanley gives this analogy: "A bodybuilder doesn't begin by lifting 500 pounds the first day. Rather, he exercises daily, gradually increasing his strength. Regularly exercising faith can bring about similar growth spiritually."[8]

In other words, do not become discouraged if you do not see results right away. I have tried raising the dead on three different occasions but was unsuccessful. Yet that does not stop me from continuing to try. I haven't seen the paralyzed rise from a wheel chair yet, but through my measure of faith, I have seen pain leave, knees healed, legs stretched, and backs straightened.

Our job is to continue to trust and seek ways to increase our faith. We can increase our measure of faith by

---

[7] Brooks, 84.

[8] Charles Stanley, In Touch Daily Devotions, http://www.intouch.org/read/magazine/daily-devotions/how-to-increase-your-faith.

praying and fasting (Luke 17:5); by reading, meditating, speaking, and obeying the word of God (Romans 10:17); and by remembering and celebrating the faithfulness of God in our life or the lives of others (1 Corinthians 10:6, 11).

Faith for the Supernatural

In Mark 11, we get a crash course from Jesus on how to see the miraculous through faith. In this portion of scripture, we see Jesus approach a fig tree because he was hungry. When He noticed there weren't figs on this tree, He cursed it and the tree withered. Later on, as the disciples looked on in astonishment, Jesus taught them how to operate in the miraculous.

Now, although the real significance of this story is about God's judgment upon Israel and its leaders, we learn a few things about how we can see supernatural things happen, like the withering of the fig tree.

If we want to see God answer our prayers, move our mountains, and perform the miraculous in our lives, we must: (1) Have faith in God (Mark 11:22). (2) Express our faith with our words and actions (Mark 11:23a; James 2:26). (3) Not doubt (Mark 11:23b). (4) Believe that it is already done (Mark 11:24).

Now, before proceeding any further, it is important that before we pray for anything, first, we must know that what we are asking is the will of God (1 John 5:14-15). Second, that our motives are correct (James 4:2-3). And third, that it is possible to receive a "yes" from God that doesn't manifest immediately (Hebrews 6:12).[9]

The importance of faith should not be under- estimated. Faith is essential to seeing the supernatural in our lives. We are not ordinary people. "Normal" Christianity is supernatural, period. God is "able to do far more abundantly beyond all that we ask or think" (Ephesians 3:20). The only thing that limits how much of God we see operating in our lives is our faith.

Trust God's word, heart, and ability. As some have said, faith is spelled "risk." So take risks, step out of your comfort zone, and allow the Holy Spirit to show you a whole new world—a world without limitation, a world where the will of God is done on the earth as it is in heaven.

---

[9] There might be times where you are tempted to believe that nothing happened when praying for someone or prophesying over someone, but there are occasions when certain healings take time to become complete. Or a prophetic word might come to pass later on. No matter what you see, hold on to the promises of God and continue to march forward. You will see the breakthrough if you do not give up (Galatians 6:9).

Hearing the Voice of God

He who has an ear, let him hear what the Spirit says to the churches. (Revelation 2:29)

Many of us desire to hear the audible voice of God as many saints in the Bible did. We want to have those great dramatic experiences that leave us with no room to doubt that God was speaking to us.

Even though I believe God can still speak in this way, this is not the normal, ordinary way in which He communicates with us. The ability to discern when God is speaking to us and what He is saying is critical to moving in the supernatural. By discerning His voice, we'll know when we have received a word of wisdom or knowledge, a prophetic message, a revelation or some instruction we must act upon.

God can speak to us through the Bible, dreams, visions, other people or circumstances in our lives. But I want to focus on the inner voice of God—His still small voice, or as Bill Hybels calls it, "the whispers of God." In order to understand and discern the "whispers" or voice of God, we must understand how He created us.

Body, Soul, and Spirit

The Bible says that human beings are tripartite, which means we are made up of three parts – body, soul, and spirit. Genesis 2:7 says, "Then the Lord God formed man of dust from the ground, and breathed into his nostrils the breath of life; and man became a living being." In other words, God made our bodies from the dust of the ground.

Then He breathed His Spirit, "the breath of life," into that clay body. And as a result, man became a living person. The word "being" is the Hebrew word *nephesh*, which also means soul.[10]

With our physical bodies, we interact with the physical world. With our souls we think, feel and make choices. Our souls are where our minds, emotions and will are located. Our spirit is what gives life to our bodies. James 2:26 says, that our bodies without our spirits are dead. Our human spirits are also the means by which we interact with the spiritual world. Some have described the human being as a, "spirit, that has a soul, that lives in a mobile home."

God Communicates with us from Spirit to Spirit

Now, why is this important to know? It is important because God is spirit (John 4:24) and when He communicates with us, He speaks to our human spirit. That's what Paul means when he says, "The Spirit Himself testifies with our spirit that we are children of God" (Romans 8:16). Once our human spirit receives this information, it then communicates that information to our soul and our soul then directs and controls our bodily responses.

So if we want to know when God is speaking to us, we must train our minds (souls) to discern His voice. That is why Paul tells us not to be "conformed to this world, but be transformed by the renewing of your mind, so that you may prove what the will of God is, that which is good and acceptable and perfect" (Romans 12:2).

---

[10] 1 Thessalonian 5:23 and Hebrews 4:12 also confirm the fact that we are made up of three parts.

God's Voice vs. Our Voice vs. Satan's Voice

So what does God's voice sound like? How do we know when He is talking to us? I like the definition Mark Virkler gives. He says, "the voice of God sounds like spontaneous words or pictures that flow into your mind from the Holy Spirit."[11] In other words, when God is speaking to your human spirit, you will receive words, impressions, thoughts, or images spontaneously in your mind from the Holy Spirit.

When *you* think, you can control the flow of your thoughts or manipulate the images you see. For example, you can choose to see a red apple or a green apple. You can choose to think about riding a bike or about what you want to do later on in the day. We can choose to think positive thoughts or negative thoughts.

When Satan speaks to us, he also implants thoughts or images spontaneously (Ephesians 6:16). But we can know when it is him because they will always reflect his own nature. The Bible says he is a liar (John 8:44), a thief, destroyer, and a killer (John 10:10); Satan is an accuser (Revelation 12:10) and a devourer (1 Peter 5:8). So when his thoughts or images enter your mind, they will always be against scripture, contrary to the truth, condemning, destructive, accusative, sinful, or worldly.

But when God speaks, His thoughts and images will always be in agreement with His nature, His will, and His word. Even if He speaks something hard, it will produce

---

[11] You can watch his YouTube videos or read his book titled, *4 Keys to Hearing God's Voice*.

conviction (John 16:8) not condemnation (John 3:17; Romans 8:1). His words will bring edification, encouragement and comfort (1 Corinthians 14:3). What God says will bring freedom not bondage (John 8:32).

This is one of the reasons why it is vital that believers know the word of God thoroughly. It will help you to discern between your thoughts and God's thoughts (Hebrews 4:12). It will help you discern between Satan's deceptions and God's truth (1 John 4:1; 1 Thessalonians 5:21). Jesus said, "My sheep hear My voice, and I know them, and they follow Me" (John 10:27).

Practical Keys for Discerning God's Voice

If you want to get better at hearing God, here is some advice based on Robert Morris' message series and book *Frequency*. First, set a place and time where you can meet with God every day. Second, be still and worship. Third, pray and read the Bible. Fourth, listen and write. Write down what you believe God might have spoken to you during your time in prayer and worship. Write down whatever impressions, feelings or images came to your mind as you spent time with Him. The more you practice these things, the better you will get at discerning when God is speaking to you.

As I stated earlier, knowing how to hear God will help you move in gifts of the Spirit such as words of wisdom or knowledge, prophecy, or discernment of spirits. Exercising faith and discerning the voice of God will open up the spiritual world to you. Now we're ready to discuss spiritual gifts and supernatural evangelism.

The Gifts of the Holy Spirit

Pursue love, yet desire earnestly spiritual gifts, but especially that you may prophesy. (1 Corinthians 14:1)

In his letter to the Corinthians, Paul makes a list of nine different gifts that are given to the body of Christ,

> [8] For to one is given the word of wisdom through the Spirit, and to another the word of knowledge according to the same Spirit; [9] to another faith by the same Spirit, and to another gifts of healing by the one Spirit, [10] and to another the effecting of miracles, and to another prophecy, and to another the distinguishing of spirits, to another *various* kinds of tongues, and to another the interpretation of tongues. (12:8-10)

He desires that the church would not be ignorant about the function and purpose of these gifts (12:1-3). He wants us to know: (1) that there are various types of gifts but they all come from the same God so that we will not belittle one another but work together and depend on one another (12:4-6); (2) that these gifts are a manifestation of the person and power of the Holy Spirit in our midst (12:7); and (3) that these gifts are given for "the common good," which means for the building up, strengthening, and equipping of the church (12:7).

In other words, by operating in these gifts we encourage our interdependence, allow the Spirit to manifest freely and end up building stronger believers. It is no wonder that Paul warned the believers in Thessalonica not to "quench the Spirit" (1 Thessalonians 5:19). The Spirit is "quenched" when we restrict, prohibit, or deny His gifts (manifestations). Everything of course should be done in a proper and orderly way (14:40). But don't confuse the Holy Spirit's order for man's dead religious order.

You Can Operate in all the Gifts

I was taught and used to believe that only Jesus, the apostles, and other special people were able to operate in all the gifts of the Spirit. I was told that each of us were given a particular gift and could only operate in another gift when the Spirit wanted or if a special anointing was present for a specific need. I was told if everyone could do so then we wouldn't need each other. I was shown scriptures like, "²⁹ All are not apostles, are they? All are not prophets, are they? All are not teachers, are they? All are not *workers of miracles*, are they? ³⁰ All do not have gifts of healings, do they? All do not speak with tongues, do they? All do not interpret, do they?" (12:29-30), as proof that we could not function in all the gifts.

But my perspective changed after understanding the following ideas. First, as I have heard Art Thomas say, just because this scripture mentions that not everyone operates in all the gifts, this does not mean that they *cannot* operate in all of them. The question "*does* everyone operate in these gifts?" is different to "*can* anyone operate in these gifts?"

Secondly, if we cannot have more spiritual gifts then the ones we initially received then why does Paul tell us to, "earnestly desire the greater gifts" (12:31) and "earnestly desire spiritual gifts, especially that you may prophesy"

(14:1)? In 1 Corinthians 14:1, "earnestly desire," is actually one Greek word, *zeloo*.[12] It means "to be jealous for" or "eager for." The imagery behind this word is actually one of boiling water. In other words, we are to be boiling with desire to operate in these gifts. So are you telling me we are to desire something, to the point of boiling, that we cannot have?

Thirdly, I understood that we were already given every gift. Ephesians 1:3 says, "Blessed *be* the God and Father of our Lord Jesus Christ, who has blessed us with every spiritual blessing in the heavenly *places* in Christ." 2 Peter 1:3 says, "seeing that His divine power has granted to us everything pertaining to life and godliness, through the true knowledge of Him who called us by His own glory and excellence." Even better is the fact that the Holy Spirit is God's gift to us and if we have Him, we have access to "every spiritual blessing" and to "everything pertaining to life and godliness."

I could go on, but I think these are enough to see that everyone and anyone who is a born-again, Spirit-filled believer can operate in these gifts. What keeps us from operating in these gifts is a lack of knowledge, desire, and faith.

In my own journey, when I was filled with the Holy Spirit at conversion, I received the gift of the word of wisdom. Eight months later I spoke in tongues. Ever since then I have prophesied, received words of knowledge, interpreted tongues, discerned spirits, and even seen God use me in healing and deliverance. I am not a "super spiritual" person. I'm a normal guy, who is crazy for Jesus and is willing

---

[12] Strong's #2206

to take risks and step out of the boat when He says "come." If I can experience these things, so can you.

If we are going to fish for men as Jesus did, we must learn how to operate in these spiritual gifts. In the succeeding chapters we will see, not only how to operate in these gifts, but also how they connect to supernatural evangelism.

Healing and Evangelism Part 1

These signs will accompany those who have believed: in My name… they will lay hands on the sick, and they will recover. (Mark 16:17, 18)

I hope that by now you are convinced or at least a little open to the idea that a full presentation of the gospel includes not only the proclamation of salvation, but a demonstration of the power of Gods kingdom. This is how Jesus did it. This is how the twelve, the seventy, and the early church did it. And this is how we should do it. We should preach the gospel and also demonstrate it by healing the sick and delivering the oppressed.

In this chapter, I want to briefly lay down a theology for healing. Not only is healing still for today, but it is also the will of God for everyone to be healed. In the next chapter, we will see what practical steps to take to begin seeing healing.

Healing and the Nature of God

Theology is the study of God. Even though we have not seen God (Exodus 33:20; John 1:18; 6:46; 1 Timothy 6:16; 1 John 4:12), we can know about Him by looking at nature and studying the scriptures (Romans 1:20; Psalm 19). Of course, the greatest revelation of who God is can actually be seen in the person of Jesus Christ (Colossians 1:15; Hebrews 1:3). As Bill Johnson says, "Jesus Christ is perfect theology."

One of the things that the Bible reveals about God is that He is immutable, which means He does not change (Exodus 3:14; Malachi 3:6; Psalm 102:25-27; James 1:17; Hebrews 13:8). He might change His mind (Exodus 32:14), He might change His methods (Jeremiah 31:31-34), but His nature, personality or essence will never change. As Robert Morris says very astutely, "if God could change, then God could become better. But because God is already perfect, God cannot change."

Now, because God is so vast, and His nature is so transcendent or beyond our understanding, He has revealed His unchanging nature through names that allow us to understand who He is and how He operates. For example, He is revealed in the Bible as Yahweh (YHWH) Jireh which means "the Lord our provider" (Genesis 22:14). In other words, it is in God's nature to provide for the needs of His people. Therefore His people can expect His provision when in need.

But one of those names is relevant to our discussion on healing. He is also called Yahweh Rapha which means "I am the Lord who heals you" (Exodus 15:26). This name, which reveals an unchanging characteristic of who God is and how He operates, supports the idea that God not only healed in the past, but He heals today, and will heal tomorrow.

Healing and the Atonement

Another evidence for the idea that God not only heals today, but it is His will to heal everyone is the atonement of Jesus Christ. The prophet Isaiah, speaking of Jesus and His sacrifice, prophesied,

Surely our griefs He Himself bore,
And our sorrows He carried;
Yet we ourselves esteemed Him stricken,
Smitten of God, and afflicted.
But He was pierced through for our trans-
gressions,
He was crushed for our iniquities;
The chastening for our well-being *fell* upon
Him,
And by His scourging we are healed. (53:4-
5)

There isn't any Christian that would argue that this passage isn't referring to the suffering of Jesus during his passion. But there are many who see this as speaking only of taking our sins in a spiritual fashion and support it by referencing 1 Peter 2:24. I would like to quote F. F. Bosworth, as he speaks about this very same passage. He says:

> The Hebrew words *choli* and *makob* have been incorrectly translated "griefs" and "sorrows." All who have taken the time to examine the original text have found what is acknowledged everywhere. These two words mean, respectively, "sicknesses" and "pains," everywhere else throughout the Old Testament. This word *choli* is interpreted "disease" and "sickness" in Deuteronomy 7:15; 28:61; 1 Kings 17:17; 2 Kings 1:2; 8:8; 2 Chronicles 16:12; 21:15; and other texts. The word *makob* is rendered "pain" in Job 14:22; 33:19; etc. Therefore the prophet is saying, in this fourth verse, "Surely he hath borne our sicknesses, and carried our pains." The reader is

> referred to any standard commentary for ad-
> ditional testimony on this point; but there is
> no better commentary than Matthew 8:16-
> 17.[13]

In other words, this text is actually saying that Jesus not only took our sins upon Himself, but also our physical sicknesses, diseases, and pain. Matthew actually quotes this passage in 8:16-17 to say Jesus fulfilled it when He was *physically* healing the sick in His ministry.

Through the pouring out of His blood we received forgiveness (spiritually) for our sins (Hebrews 9:22). But through the whips and physical mistreatment of His body, we received healing (physically) for our sicknesses (Isaiah 53:4-5).

Healing and the Ministry of Jesus

As I quoted earlier, "Jesus Christ is perfect theology." In other words, if we want to know the heart of God and His will all we need to do is look at Jesus. He represented the Father perfectly. Jesus said, "if you knew Me, you would know My Father also" (John 8:19). "I and the Father are one" (John 10:30). "He who has seen Me has seen the Father" (John 14:9).

Speaking of His Father's will, Jesus also said, ""Very truly I tell you, the Son can do nothing by himself; he can do only what he sees his Father doing, because whatever the Father does the Son also does" (John 5:19). So what did Jesus do during His earthly ministry that His Father was also doing? According to the following scriptures, Jesus healed everyone who came to Him for healing (Mt

---

[13] *Christ the Healer* (Grand Rapids, MI: Chosen Books, 2008), 34.

4:24; 8:16; 9:35; 12:15; 14:35-36; Mk 6:56; Lk 4:40; 6:18b-19; Acts 10:38). Did you know that Jesus never sent someone away sick that came asking for healing? This included people who wouldn't even thank Him or end up following Him (Luke 17:11-19).[14]

Healing is one of the love languages of God. He didn't always do it to create a convert. But He did want to demonstrate He loved them because "God is love" (1 John 4:8).

Healing and Forgiveness

It is also interesting to note that the idea of spiritual and physical healing frequently go together in scripture. David said in Psalm 103:3 that God forgives *all* of our sins and heals *all* of our diseases. In the Gospels, Jesus forgives the sins of a paralyzed man and then heals him of his physical condition (Matthew 9:2-8). James 5:14-16 says,

> [14] Is anyone among you sick? *Then* he must call for the elders of the church and they are to pray over him, anointing him with oil in the name of the Lord; [15] and the prayer offered in faith will restore the one who is sick, and the Lord will raise him up, and if he has committed sins, they will be forgiven him. [16] Therefore, confess your sins to one another, and pray for one another so that you may be healed. The effective prayer of a righteous man can accomplish much.

---

[14] Notice that only one leper from the 10 who were healed returned to thank Jesus.

Not all sicknesses are related to a specific sin, but the point is that regardless of your need, whether for spiritual or physical healing, it is God's will to do both.

Healing and Salvation

In addition to this, even within the Greek word for salvation, *sozo*, is the idea of deliverance for the complete person.[15] The word can be translated save, heal, rescue or deliver. So God is interested in saving, healing, rescuing, and delivering us both spiritually and physically. Even more important, God desires this to be our reality today. The Bible says, "now is 'the acceptable time,' behold, now is 'the day of salvation'" (2 Corinthians 6:2). God wants to "sanctify you entirely; and may your spirit and soul and body be preserved complete" (1 Thessalonians 5:23).

So is it God's will to forgive sins today? Is it God's will to save sinners today? Then it is also God's will to heal today. No exceptions.[16]

Healing and Human Nature

Another evidence that God is willing to heal today is our human body. When is the last time you have gotten cut? Or when is the last time you have gotten a cold? Have you noticed that your body automatically has a process to try and heal you?

---

[15] Strong's #4982

[16] You might be thinking, "If it is God's will to heal everyone today, then why isn't everyone healed?" For the same reason not everyone is saved. Not everyone will come to God or trust God for their healing. Every single person who came to Jesus for healing in the gospels was healed, without exception. Jesus hasn't changed.

If you get cut, all of a sudden blood begins to flow to the area where there is an open wound. Your blood then forms a protective layer to cover the exposed area. The body then begins to repair broken vessels and create new skin or tissue. When the process is over, depending on how small the wound is, you're as good as new.

Or if you get a cold, your body works towards creating homeostasis. The antibodies and your immune system begin to fight out off any germs or infections. Your body also creates certain proteins to strengthen you and heal you.

God built us to heal and survive. This is a grace that is given to mankind even if they reject God and never come to Him. The healing process is natural, but it reflects the heart, intention and desire of a supernatural God.

Healing and Human Efforts

What about hospitals and medicine? God has provided healing elements within nature itself to help bring physical health and healing. On top of the natural foods and plants doctors can use, they also have created procedures to try and help people who are hurting, sick or in pain. Are you telling me doctors and nurses have more compassion then God?

Matter of fact, let me ask you an even better question. If it is not always God's will to heal you, then why do you go to the doctors? Why do you seek help for your sicknesses, diseases and pain? If God wants some people to be sick, and then they go to the doctors for help, would they not be in disobedience? As Art Thomas says, "if it is not God's will to heal everyone, then why did Jesus go around healing all the sick? Was He going against the Father's will?"[17]

I think this is really obvious. If it is in God's unchanging nature to heal, if healing was a part of the atonement of Jesus, if healing and forgiveness are two sides of one coin, if all of nature points towards healing, then how can anyone think that God does not heal today and that even if He did, it is not always His will to do so?

I believe it is because we have allowed our experiences, traditions and biases to inform our faith instead of the word of God. I am convinced by the word of God that God still heals today. I am convinced by the word of God that *it is His will* to heal everyone today. I am even more convinced that God is willing to use you and me to heal if we will let Him.

---

[17] "10 Things Jesus Never Said About Healing," YouTube video, 1:10:21, posted by Art Thomas, February 1, 2014, https://www.youtube.com/watch?v=hHDKlfcbn2g.

Healing and Evangelism Part 2

These signs will accompany those who have believed: in My name... they will lay hands on the sick, and they will recover. (Mark 16:17, 18)

Part of the Great Commission is to teach believers to obey everything that Jesus has commanded. Did you know that part of the commands of Jesus to His disciples included healing the sick? "[7] And as you go, preach, saying, 'The kingdom of heaven is at hand.' [8] Heal *the* sick, raise *the* dead, cleanse *the* lepers, cast out demons. Freely you received, freely give" (Matthew 10:7-8). Did you know that in the same context of the Great Commission, Jesus said that believers would lay hands on the sick and that they would be healed as a sign to confirm the message of the gospel of the kingdom? (Mark 16:17-18).

There are many who say, "yeah, but Jesus said these signs would follow believers, not that believers should be following these signs." I love Bill Johnson's response to this idea. He says, "Well, are the signs following you? If not, follow the signs until the signs begin to follow you." If the signs are not following us then we must learn why and how to begin seeing the supernatural in our lives. That is the purpose of this chapter, to learn how to begin to heal the sick.

In my observations, I have noticed that there isn't any one formula to heal the sick. There are some places where Jesus lays hands on the sick (Luke 4:40). In other instances He would just give a word (Luke 7:1-10). There are times where He would do strange things like spit or apply mud to people's eyes (Mark 7:33; 8:23; John 9:6). Peter even saw healing at times when his shadow would pass over people (Acts 5:15). Others were healed with handkerchiefs that came from Paul's body (Acts 19:12).

The point of all these examples is to say that there is not just one way to see people healed. But what I would like to do is give you some steps that can get you started in seeing the sick healed. The more people you pray for, the more people you will see healed. The opposite is also true. If you never pray for anyone, you will never see God use you to heal.

Step #1 – Interview the Person

We must always remember that whatever we do must be done in a spirit of love. "Love builds up" (1 Corinthians 8:1). So we do not want to just start going up to strangers and laying hands on them, we want to build a bridge that allows them to feel comfortable for us to pray for them. That bridge is the interview.

I've heard people say, "no one cares how much you know, until they know how much you care." Conversing and asking people questions can demonstrate you are interested.

The interview is also helpful because it helps you to know what exactly is going on with the person and therefore determine how you will pray for them. You don't want to be casting demons out of someone when it might just be something natural. Similarly, you don't want to pray as if it's something natural when there might be a spiritual reason behind their sickness or pain. That's what the interview is for. Here are some questions you can ask them:

- How are you doing today? How are you feeling?
- I notice that you're in pain; what's wrong? Can I pray for you?
- How long have you been sick or had this pain?
- Can you remember what might have been happening at this time in your life when you started feeling the first symptoms?
- What do you feel right now? On a scale of 1 to 10, how much pain do you have right now?

Depending on how much time you have with the person, you can decide which questions to ask them. Depending on how they answer, you will have an idea of how to pray for them later.

Step #2 – Place your Hands on the Affected Area

Now, before you put your hands on anyone, make sure they are okay with it and that it is appropriate for you to do so. If you're a man, and you're praying for a woman, the safest places to lay your hands is on their head, shoulders, or hands. If they are okay with it, you can also place your hands on their knees or their ankles if that is the affected area. The point is to do everything in purity and love. When possible, let women pray for women and men for men.

Now one reason we want to lay our hands on them is because this is an example we see in Jesus, the apostles and the early church. In Mark 16:18, it actually even says to lay hands and they will recover.

Another reason we lay our hands is because physical touch can sometimes communicate trust, love, or compassion. There are some people who don't normally receive a loving touch from family or friends, much less a stranger. Jesus healed a leper in Matthew 8:2-3, but before doing so He touched him. It wasn't necessary, but when was the last time that man was touched by anyone?

Lastly, I believe we should lay hands because power can sometimes be transferred by touch (see Mark 5:25-34).

Step #3 – Invite the Presence of the Holy Spirit

It wasn't Peter's shadow or Paul's handkerchief or Jesus' spit that healed the sick; it was the presence of the Holy Spirit. The power of God to heal is in the Holy Spirit (Acts 1:8). The power to demonstrate the kingdom of God is in the Holy Spirit (Matthew 12:28). When we ask Him to come over the individual, it allows the person to feel God's presence, love, and power for themselves. These types of encounters with God cannot be underestimated.

Many times when the Holy Spirit is working in the person they might begin to feel heat, electricity, tingling, or just a sense of peace. These are very good signs that God is actually working in the person and you can let them know that. It also encourages your own faith to know they are feeling something.

I prayed for a young lady on one occasion. The length of her legs were uneven. After praying, her shorter leg stretched and she began crying. When I spoke with her grandmother a day later, I was told that her legs were still tingling the rest of that day.

The feelings are not mandatory, they're an encouragement. Of course, there are going to be times when the person doesn't feel anything and still get healed. But no matter what, trust God and allow His presence to work in the person. The more we cooperate with Him, the more healing we'll see.

Step #4 – Command any Spirits to Leave and the Body to Heal

Did you know that I could not find one example where Jesus, the apostles, or the early church actually asked God to heal someone? This is not to contradict the earlier step, but Jesus told us to heal the sick. Now, of course, we recognize that we cannot heal anyone. It is God who heals. But I believe the point is that Christ has given us authority to act on His behalf.

The Bible says, "And He called the twelve together, and gave them power and authority over all the demons and to heal diseases" (Luke 9:1). And with that authority, we command spirits of pain or sickness to leave and we command bones, joints, nerves, tendons, or muscles to heal.

We must command because authority is expressed through our words. The centurion who asked Jesus to heal his servant recognized this.

> [6] Now Jesus *started* on His way with them; and when He was not far from the house, the centurion sent friends, saying to Him, "Lord, do not trouble Yourself further, for I am not worthy for You to come under my roof; [7] for this reason I did not even consider myself worthy to come to You, but *just* say the word,

and my servant will be healed. [8] For I also am a man placed under authority, with soldiers under me; and I say to this one, 'Go!' and he goes, and to another, 'Come!' and he comes, and to my slave, 'Do this!' and he does it." [9] Now when Jesus heard this, He marveled at him, and turned and said to the crowd that was following Him, "I say to you, not even in Israel have I found such great faith." [10] When those who had been sent returned to the house, they found the slave in good health. (Luke 7:6-10)

Using the authority given to us by Jesus, we should command healing to occur. Art Thomas says (and I'm paraphrasing) that asking God to heal someone that He has already told you to heal is like you asking someone to get you a cup of water and when they get the cup they turn around and ask you to come fill the cup and get the water!

Also allow me to give you this advice, don't pray long prayers. It's not about how many words you say. It's about praying and commanding with faith. Notice the commands in the Bible, "rise up," "pick up your mat and go," "eye's open."

Step #5 – Thank God for what He is Doing in the Person

The Bible says that God "inhabits the praise of His people" (Psalm 22:3 NIV). Thanking God for what He is doing increases the manifestation of His presence. It also takes everyone's eyes off of what is happening with the person and focuses them on God. Thankfulness also reflects humility because it reminds everyone that God is the one doing the work. "We are unworthy slaves; we have done *only* that which we ought to have done" (Luke 17:10).

Step #6 – Ask the person to do something they couldn't do before

The Bible says "that faith without works is dead" (James 2:17, 26). By having the person move in faith, you are inviting them to be a part of their process of healing. You won't know what has occurred if the person doesn't test it. There are times that people won't feel anything while you are praying but when they try to move that shoulder, or walk with that knee, or rise up from their wheelchair, they will find that they were already healed.

In Acts 3 we find this to be the case with the man that Peter and John prayed for. The Bible says, "[7] And seizing him by the right hand, he raised him up; and immediately his feet and his ankles were strengthened. [8] With a leap he stood upright and *began* to walk; and he entered the temple with them, walking and leaping and praising God" (3:7-8). Notice that his ankles were strengthened after faith was put into action and not before.

This can sometimes be the most intimidating moment. Our first instinct is to pray and then walk away before anyone notices that maybe nothing happened. I know, I have done that many times. But we must cross "the chicken line" and see what has happened. We are not in this for our image, reputation or glory. We are here to glorify and obey God.

Know this, even if nothing happens, people will appreciate the fact that you took time to pray for them. The gesture of prayer is a gesture that will communicate love.

Some people will be incredulous from the start, so you can't lose. If you pray and nothing happens, the people still walk away feeling loved. If you pray and something does happen, the people leave with joy, feeling loved by God and now they are more open to hearing about Jesus. It's a win-win situation.

What to do if Nothing Happens

Faith is stubborn. It does not give up. So if the person allows you, try again and again until God does something. I have had many instances where I have seen a person healed after praying three or four times. Start the process over. Ask them if they felt anything during the prayer. Some will tell you they began to feel heat or tingling or a sense of peace. Some might tell you they felt their pain increase or move to another part of their body. This is a sign there is a demon causing their pain. Lay hands on the person, ask the Spirit to come upon the person, command the spirit or spirits to leave and command whatever the affected area is to be healed. Then praise God for what He is doing and then have them check out their body again.

Repeat these steps as many times as necessary. Remember it is God's will for them to be healed and He wants to use you. Did you know there were times where even Jesus had to pray more than once for someone to be healed? (see Mark 8:23-25). So if Jesus needed to pray more than once at times, you and I can definitely pray seven or eight times for a person to be healed. The point is, don't give up. God is with you and you will see results if you continue to push through.

Deliverance and Evangelism Part 1

These signs will accompany those who have believed: in My name they will cast out demons... (Mark 16:17)

Each of the chapters in this book can be turned into a whole book. The topic of deliverance is one of those topics where hundreds of books, seminars, and videos have been done in order to inform God's people. Even among these, there are differences in methods and ideologies. I am not trying to give you an exhaustive explanation of everything, just an overview to get you started.[18]

I would like to begin by giving you some fundamental truths before engaging in spiritual warfare.

1. Christ is our Focus, not Satan

The Bible is very clear on where our eyes, heart, and mind should be focused. The Bible says, "fixing our eyes on Jesus, the author and perfecter of faith" (Hebrews 12:2). "Therefore if you have been raised up with Christ, keep seeking the things above, where Christ is, seated at the right hand of God. ² Set your mind on the things above, not on the things that are on earth. ³ For you have died and your life is hidden with Christ in God" (Colossians 3:1-3). "⁸ Finally, brethren, whatever is true, whatever is honorable, whatever is right, whatever is pure, whatever is lovely, whatever is of good repute, if there is any excellence and if

---

[18] If you want to look at any of these topics more in depth, I will recommend material at the end of this book to help you in your research.

anything worthy of praise, dwell on these things" (Philippians 4:8).

I have seen many people become so devil-conscious that they see him in every corner. Constantly on their lips are words like, "the devil did this," "the devil said that," "the devil made me do this or that," etc. Satan is a real person, but he is not our focus—Jesus is. The closer we get to Christ and the more we know God, the more we will see victory over the forces of darkness. "Submit therefore to God. Resist the devil and he will flee from you" (James 4:7).

2. Know what Christ has Accomplished and Who we are in Him

We will not be very effective in spiritual warfare or deliverance if we do not know what Christ has accomplished and what He has made available to us through our relationship with Him. The Bible says, "My people are destroyed for lack of knowledge" (Hosea 4:6). Understanding these truths will keep us from falling prey to the devil's lies and schemes.

First, we must understand that by the death and resurrection of Jesus, Satan has suffered defeat and has lost his authority to operate in the earthly realm (Luke 4:6; John 12:31). God promised in Genesis 3:15 that one day Jesus would "crush" the head of Satan, the ancient serpent (Revelation 12:9). God began the fulfillment of this promise with the crucifixion of Jesus, so that through His "death He might render powerless him who had the power of death, that is, the devil" (Hebrews 2:14). "And having disarmed the powers and authorities, he made a public spectacle of them, triumphing over them by the cross" (Colossians 2:15 NIV).

So now the devil operates in this present world illegally. That is why when Christ resurrected and ascended into heaven He passed on to us the work He started. Along with the job of casting Satan out, He has also given us complete authority over the spiritual world. The Bible says that God,

> ...raised Him from the dead and seated Him at His right hand in the heavenly *places*, [21] far above all rule and authority and power and dominion, and every name that is named, not only in this age but also in the one to come. [22] And He put all things in subjection under His feet, and gave Him as head over all things to the church, [23] which is His body, the fullness of Him who fills all in all. (Ephesians 1:20-23)

God also "raised us up with Him, and seated us with Him in the heavenly *places* in Christ Jesus" (Ephesians 2:6). Jesus has also given us "power and authority over all the demons and to heal diseases" (Luke 9:1). He also said "Behold, I have given you authority to tread on serpents and scorpions, and over all the power of the enemy, and nothing will injure you" (Luke 10:19).

In other words, by being in Christ, we share in His authority. The same authority that Jesus exercised when on earth, He has given to us. We are "little" Christs in this world. Because He lives, both in heaven and in us through the Holy Spirit, we have all the support and resources of heaven at our disposal.

3. We Fight *from* Victory not *for* Victory

Understanding that Jesus has already defeated and disarmed Satan, and that He has given us the same authority to continue doing so, allows us to confront the enemy with confidence. It helps us to understand that we are not fighting to win a war. We have already won the war. We are fighting *from* victory not *for* victory. We are enforcing the victory Christ has already won through His death and resurrection. You can call yourself a "Kingdom Enforcer."

Wherever we go, we enforce the will and kingdom of God over the kingdom of darkness. So when we minister to a person we are not wondering if we have enough authority or anointing to help them. We have all authority.

It is like what happened during World War 2. The war was won long before Hitler died. Even though the war was won, there were still rebel groups that resisted the Allies. But those rebels were not in authority anymore. Those rebels had lost, but the army kept moving in until the victory was enforced and completed.

One day we will see the same thing. There is a day coming when Satan and his demons will be cast into the lake of fire (Matthew 25:41; Revelation 20:10) and then there will be a New Heaven and a New Earth (Revelation 21:1) where "He will wipe away every tear from their eyes; and there will no longer be *any* death; there will no longer be *any* mourning, or crying, or pain; the first things have passed away" (Revelation 21:4).

But until then we will fight from victory and continue casting out demons and tearing down strongholds in order to set people free.

4. We are in a Real Spiritual War

In the rationalistic and naturalistic mindsets of many people, the reality of the involvement of the devil in our daily lives gets either ignored or completely denied. C. S. Lewis said (and I am paraphrasing) that there were two great errors people can commit when it came to the devil. The first is to overemphasize him and the other is to completely disbelieve in his existence.

The Bible says there is such a person as Satan. He is known as the ancient serpent, the great dragon or the devil (Revelation 12:9). He is known as an accuser (Revelation 12:10), a thief, killer and destroyer (John 10:10). He is known as a liar and the Father of lies (John 8:44). The Bible also calls him "the prince of the power of the air" (Ephesians 2:2).

This evil personality is not somewhere bound and uninvolved. No, the Bible says that he is currently the god (with a little "g") of this world and has "blinded the minds of the unbelieving so that they might not see the light of the gospel of the glory of Christ, who is the image of God" (2 Corinthians 4:4). "The whole world lies in the power of the evil one" (1 John 5:19).

Now, he doesn't rule the world by himself. He has a kingdom, a militant army of demons, an organized rebel group of fallen angels (Matthew 12:26; Ephesians 6:12). Satan, together with his forces of evil work in the children of disobedience (Ephesians 2:2). They tempt, oppress, afflict, torment, and deceive.

Yes, they are defeated but they are still active in the world rebelling against the kingdom of God. Our job is to enforce the kingdom of God. That is why it is important to be informed on who your enemy is and how he operates. "Be of sober *spirit*, be on the alert. Your adversary, the devil, prowls around like a roaring lion, seeking someone to devour" (1 Peter 5:8).

In the next chapter we will see how fighting this enemy fits in with winning souls and affirming them in the kingdom of God.

Deliverance and Evangelism Part 2

These signs will accompany those who have believed: in My name they will cast out demons... (Mark 16:17)

When we mention the term "spiritual warfare," we are referring to the fight and struggle that exists between the kingdom of God and the kingdom of Satan. These two kingdoms are not two opposite equal powers. No, God is sovereign and is omnipotent. He reigns over the whole universe. Satan is a defeated foe who is in rebellion to God's will.

But this fight includes a third party – humanity. Both God and Satan seek to reign and establish their kingdom in the hearts of man. God does it through love and Satan through manipulation. God does it through truth and Satan through deception. God is willing to lay down His life to set the prisoners free, while Satan is willing to take life in order to keep people in bondage.

It is because of this struggle for the hearts of men that spiritual warfare is taking place here on earth and not somewhere in space. God is now taking back what Satan usurped by giving His authority to us, the Church. As the Church, we fight this war with both defensive and offensive strategies and weapons.

1. Spiritual Warfare of Believers

Because the Church walks in the same authority and power that Jesus did when He was here on earth, the enemy seeks ways to keep us from being effective. He uses lies, deception and open doors to try and gain access into our lives so that we will not walk in the fullness of the character, love and power of Jesus Christ to set others free.

For example, Paul says that holding onto anger can give access to the devil, "[26] Be angry, and *yet* do not sin; do not let the sun go down on your anger, [27] and do not give the devil an opportunity" (Ephesians 4:26-27). Jesus said that those who hold on to unforgiveness and bitterness will be tormented, "[34] And his lord, moved with anger, handed him over to the torturers until he should repay all that was owed him. [35] My heavenly Father will also do the same to you, if each of you does not forgive his brother from your heart" (Matthew 18:34-35).

So we have been given a mighty, powerful and effective strategy in order to keep ourselves from being taken advantage of by the enemy. The strategy is called a life of holiness. A sanctified and consecrated life is the best defense of a believer against the enemy. This truth is illustrated in what Paul calls the "armor of God."

> [10] Finally, be strong in the Lord and in the strength of His might. [11] Put on the full armor of God, so that you will be able to stand firm against the schemes of the devil. [12] For our struggle is not against flesh and blood, but against the rulers, against the powers, against the world forces of this darkness, against the spiritual forces of wickedness in the heavenly places. [13] Therefore, take up the full armor of God, so that you will be able to resist in the

evil day, and having done everything, to stand firm. (Ephesians 6:10-13)

When you read the rest of the chapter, you will notice he mentions elements of that armor that will help us stand firm against the schemes or attacks of the devil. He speaks of walking in truth (honesty and transparency), righteousness (integrity and obedience), peace, salvation (assurance of our position in God), faith, word of God, and prayer (see Ephesians 6:14-18).

James summarizes this best in one sentence, "[7] Submit therefore to God. Resist the devil and he will flee from you" (James 4:7). How can we help set the captives free if we are captive ourselves? Let us walk in freedom, and then we will be able to help others be free also.

2. Spiritual Warfare in a Region

If you travel to different parts of the world, or even different cities or states you will notice that certain sins are more dominant in one place than another. The reason for this is the demonic powers that are operating in that region. The Bible calls them "principalities, rulers or powers" (Ephesians 6:12). These are demonic princes' who have been delegated authority over specific geographical areas. A great example of this can be seen in the story of Daniel.

In Daniel 10, Daniel determines to pray and ask God for an answer about something he was concerned about. God sent him the answer with an angel immediately after he began praying, but the angel was detained by one of these principalities.

"[12] Then he said to me, 'Do not be afraid, Daniel, for from the first day that you set your heart on understanding *this* and on humbling yourself before your God, your words were heard, and I have come in response to your words. [13] But the prince of the kingdom of Persia was withstanding me for twenty-one days; then behold, Michael, one of the chief princes, came to help me, for I had been left there with the kings of Persia. [14] Now I have come to give you an understanding of what will happen to your people in the latter days, for the vision pertains to the days yet *future*.'" (Daniel 10:12-14)

So we can see from this example that many times believers will experience opposition from these types of spirits whenever they are attempting to do the will of God.

By looking at the New Testament, one of the way to overcome principalities and demonic spirits over regions is through the conversion of the masses by power evangelism. We can see this clearly in three different examples. But I will only speak on the first.[19] In Luke 10 Jesus sends out 70 disciples to preach the kingdom, cast out demons and heal the sick. This is what happens when they returned from their short mission trip:

[17] The seventy returned with joy, saying, "Lord, even the demons are subject to us in Your name." [18] And He said to them, "I was

---

[19] The other two examples can be found in the book of Acts, chapters eight and nineteen. As the gospel goes forth in both of these regions of Samaria and Ephesus, the principalities of witchcraft and paganism begin to crumble as people come to Christ in large numbers. Another mighty way to overcome these territorial spirits is through prayer, fasting, and intercession.

watching Satan fall from heaven like lightning. [19] Behold, I have given you authority to tread on serpents and scorpions, and over all the power of the enemy, and nothing will injure you. [20] Nevertheless do not rejoice in this, that the spirits are subject to you, but rejoice that your names are recorded in heaven. (v17-20)

So as the 70 are preaching, casting out demons, and healing the sick people are converting and the spiritual forces of wickedness are losing their authority.

There are many who would differ with me with this point of how to conduct regional or territorial warfare but I see no reason to fear going into a region because of what power might be operating there. Yes we want to pray; yes, we want to be informed of what we will be dealing with. But Jesus already said, "Go into all the world and preach the gospel" (Mark 16:15). We have been given authority over all the power of the enemy. So "Go!"

The more sinners are converted, the more these spirits will lose their influence and power over the region.

3. Spiritual Warfare for Unbelievers

I would like to propose two ideas when it comes to unbelievers. First, do not expect every battle to be as dramatic as what is seen in the Exorcist movies. Spiritual warfare does not have to last hours and hours. "[16] When evening came, they brought to Him many who were demon-possessed; and He cast out the spirits with a word, and healed all who were ill." (Matthew 8:16). Notice, "He cast out the spirits with a word."

In many instances, just commanding the spirits to leave will be sufficient. You can say "In Jesus name, I bind any unclean spirit and command you to leave this body right now." Or "I command any spirit of pain to loosen this person, and come out right now." There are some cases where you will have to be a little more persistent. But if you stay in faith, they will eventually come out.

The second idea I would like to propose is that if an unbeliever is under the oppression of a more serious, violent or stubborn demon that is afflicting the persons soul, do not deliver them unless they are willing to surrender their lives to Jesus. This might sound cruel, but hear me out. Jesus said,

> [24] When the unclean spirit goes out of a man, it passes through waterless places seeking rest, and not finding any, it says, 'I will return to my house from which I came.' [25] And when it comes, it finds it swept and put in order. [26] Then it goes and takes *along* seven other spirits more evil than itself, and they go in and live there; and the last state of that man becomes worse than the first. (Luke 11:24-26)

In other words, if you are able to deliver a person who is not willing to surrender their lives to Jesus,[20] those spirits will come back later with more spirits and the person will be worse. It is the presence of the Holy Spirit in us that

---

[20] Some may question if this is even possible. Believers have been given authority over all demons by Jesus and we can cast out spirits even without the person asking. That can be seen in the example of the girl with a spirit of divination (Acts 16:18).

gives us power to overcome sin, temptation and the devil. If the Holy Spirit is not in us, as can be seen in the example Jesus gave, who will keep those spirits from returning in greater numbers or force?

In his book, *The Biblical Guidebook to Deliverance*, Randy Clark says, "If someone is not a believer and wishes to receive deliverance, we can lead them to the Lord before we minister deliverance, or we can expel the demon and then lead them to Christ immediately afterward. Either way works."[21]

Randy Clark recommends when ministering deliverance that,

1. ***We must understand that the person is the priority.*** We must make sure to minister to the person in love. They are not the demon, they are being oppressed by one.
2. ***We must take authority over any manifestations.*** Although many believe that we should speak to the demons in order to get information to help the person, I would advise the contrary. Demons are liars, and whatever we need to help the person can be received through the Holy Spirit.[22] It is not loving to allow the demon to use, control or manipulate the person just because we think it will help. Let us not allow them to humiliate the person anymore. Command the spirit to submit, or be silent in Jesus name.

---

[21] Clark, 48. Kindle Edition; If you want to know more about this idea you can read his book, especially chapter 5. I will also list different resources on this topic of deliverance at the end of this book.

[22] We should pray for the gift of the discernment of spirits. This is the ability to know the name or nature of the spirit working in a person or environment through one or more of our spiritual senses.

3. *We should determine the person's sincerity.* Does the person really want to be free? If not the spirits will have an open door in order to get back into their lives.

4. *We should determine if they have accepted or are willing to accept Christ as their Lord and Savior.* If they haven't and are unwilling to accept Him, we should lovingly encourage them to reconsider. If they insist then we should bless them and pray that God would work in their lives. If they haven't, but are willing, we should help them pray to receive Christ.

5. *We should interview them to help them close any doors that has given the enemy access to their lives.* I would recommend taking the person through a process formed by Neil Anderson in his book, *The Steps to Freedom in Christ.*[23] But if you don't have access to this material, have them confess whatever sins they have committed or doors they might have opened to the enemy. Some areas you can begin with are: involvement in the occult, people they have been hurt by and need to forgive, ways they might be in rebellion towards authority, or sins of lust, pride, or greed. Then have them repent and renounce those sins. For example, "Lord I confess I am guilty of (name the sin). I no longer want this in my life and I renounce it in the name of Jesus. Forgive me and cleanse me with your blood. In Jesus name, amen."

---

[23] This process takes a couple hours, but it is worth it to set the person free. If you would like to get more familiar with his steps, please read *Victory Over the Darkness, Bondage Breaker,* and *Discipleship Counseling.* These are all books by Neil Anderson.

6. ***We should then cast out these spirits and invite the Holy Spirit to fill them.*** Once the person has gone through the steps of confessing and repenting of any sins or doors that gave the enemy a right to their lives, the demonic spirits no longer have a right to be there. At this point we can command them to leave, and then ask Jesus to fill them with the Holy Spirit.

These are just guidelines. These principles are not written in stone. Please pray, study the Bible, read other materials and allow the Holy Spirit to give you your own convictions. But whatever you do, do not remain ignorant of this topic. Do not become indifferent to those in need of deliverance.

If we want to fish for men and enforce the kingdom, we must know our enemy; we must know how to live victoriously over his strategies; and we must know how to help others get free of his oppression.

Words of Knowledge and Evangelism

⁷ But to each one is given the manifestation of the Spirit for the common good. ⁸ For to one is given the word of wisdom through the Spirit, and to another the word of knowledge according to the same Spirit (1 Corinthians 12:7, 8)

After healing and deliverance, one of the supernatural signs that can be the most useful in winning the lost to Jesus is the gift of the word of knowledge. Art Thomas says a word of knowledge is "when the Holy Spirit takes something Jesus knows and reveals it to us."[24] In his book Divine Healing Made Simple, Praying Medic defines a word of knowledge as "information given by the Holy Spirit revealing certain facts, which God is aware of, but we are not. It is information about a past or present situation that is true."[25]

In other words, this gift is the ability to hear or receive specific information from God about something or someone that is or was true. If it is something that you know through natural wisdom, investigation or discernment then that is not a word of knowledge. For it to be a word of knowledge it must be true, it must be about someone's past or present, and it must be something you had no prior knowledge of.

---

[24] *The Word of Knowledge in Action*, 41. Kindle Edition.
[25] Praying Medic, Location 1642 of 3918. Kindle Edition.

Words of Knowledge in the Ministry of Christ

Jesus operated in this gift in order to reach the lost. In John chapter 4 Jesus encounters a Samaritan woman at a well. After conversing with her over water He says this to her, "'Go, call your husband and come here.' [17] The woman answered and said, 'I have no husband.' Jesus said to her, 'You have correctly said, "I have no husband"; [18] for you have had five husbands, and the one whom you now have is not your husband; this you have said truly'" (4:16-18).

Now, how could Jesus have known this about this woman? He had never met her before. This was the first time he was conversing with her. And there were no natural clues to inform Jesus of this woman's present and past. It could only have been revealed to Him by the Holy Spirit.

This was her response, "Sir, I perceive that You are a prophet" (4:19). From this moment on, she was open to hear what He had to say about more spiritual things. Eventually, Jesus revealed Himself as the Messiah, she accepted this truth, and brought a whole city to come and meet Jesus for themselves. All this from one word of knowledge!

This wasn't the only instance where something like this happened. A word of knowledge helped bring a man named Zacchaeus to repentance (Luke 19:1-10). A word of knowledge also helped draw in one of his disciples named Nathanael (John 1:43-51).

Words of knowledge have the ability to peek someone's interest and curiosity. A word of knowledge can help confirm the validity of a prophetic word or even the message or ministry of a person. A word of knowledge can even increase faith in God and His ability to do what He promised.

How can we Receive Words of Knowledge?

Anyone can receive a word of knowledge, because this gift really depends on our ability to hear God and discern His voice. And since the Holy Spirit lives in us we can all hear God for ourselves. The amount and the accuracy of the words of knowledge we receive depend on our sensitivity to the Spirit, our knowledge of how He speaks and our willingness to obey and speak what we have received.

If we walk in the flesh, it will be difficult to discern when God is speaking to us. If we are ignorant of how words of knowledge are given, we won't know when we are receiving one. If we don't act upon the words we do receive then why should He give us more?

In his book, *Words of Knowledge*, Randy Clark speaks of six different ways that words of knowledge can come to us. You can feel them, read them, see them, think them, say them, or dream them. This is not an exhaustive list, but they are the main ways people receive words of knowledge.

1. Feel it

Randy Clark says, "It comes as a physical, sympathetic pain that you can literally feel in your body. It is not a pain that you would normally have on your own."[26] In other words, God allows you to feel in your own body what someone else may be feeling in theirs. So you can be praying for someone or ministering in a church or just walking

---

[26] Clark, Location 106 of 802. Kindle Edition.

somewhere and all of a sudden you start to feel a pain on the left side of your head, or on one of your ankles, or in your chest. That pain wasn't there before, and there is no natural reason for you to feel the way you do. This can sometimes be a word of knowledge of what someone else is feeling or experiencing.

In a case like this, you can ask either the person you are ministering to or the church in general if there is someone experiencing that specific situation. If anyone says yes, it is a confirmation that God gave you a word of knowledge and that He wants you to pray for that specific problem because He is actually going to change it.

2. Read it

This happens when you can "literally see the words spelled out – even sometimes you can see them on people. You literally see words just going across in front of your eyes. For some people, it's like a big newspaper headline going across in front of them. For other people it's like ticker tape, like on the stock market, just going across – and they can actually read it just like they were reading."[27] Clark mentions that those who receive words of knowledge in such a fashion usually are more accurate. A person who moved powerfully in this way is William Branham.

3. See it

When words of knowledge come in this fashion, "you see them – you don't read them, but you see them."[28] They are like mental pictures. You might see images or mini "movies" playing in your mind's eye. This is the way

---

[27] Ibid, Location 170 of 802. Kindle Edition.
[28] Ibid, Location 220 of 802. Kindle Edition.

I normally receive words of knowledge. I'll see pictures and when I speak what I see the person will usually confirm what I am saying to be true.

4. Think it

Words of knowledge might come also as thoughts or impressions in your mind. A word, name, or a situation may pop up in your mind about the person.

5. Say it

Have you ever been speak or praying for someone and all of sudden words begin to flow from your mouth that you didn't know or weren't expecting to say? Then all of a sudden the person might begin to cry, or get emotional or express being surprised because you mentioned something that they were feeling, or had gone through that no one else or a few people knew.

Words of knowledge can also come in this way. Randy Clark calls it "inspired speech."[29] He says "you don't think about saying, or even plan to say it, it just happened to come out of your mouth. You actually hear it for the first time yourself when you speak it out… It bypasses the cognitive processes of the brain."[30]

6. Dream it

Information about people or things that are currently going on or have occurred can also be revealed in dreams. God may show us the condition, problem, sin, or need of

---

[29] Ibid, Location 427 of 802. Kindle Edition.
[30] Ibid, Location 427-437 of 802. Kindle Edition.

someone else. When we share the dream with that person, they confirm it to be true.

Love and Wisdom when Receiving and Giving Words of Knowledge

Those are six ways that words of knowledge can come to an individual. Besides knowing how they come, we must also know what to do with them. For that we need love and wisdom.

It is important to remember that the gifts of the Holy Spirit are for building people up, not for tearing them down. If you receive a word of knowledge of someone's sin or problem, don't share it with anyone else. If God is showing it to you it is because He wants to use you to pray for that person and express His love towards them in whatever their situation is.

Don't use words of knowledge to bring condemnation to a person if it is something negative. God will test us to see how we use the information He gives us. If we can't be trusted with a little, He won't give us more. The more you lovingly and wisely use His gifts, the more He will allow you to experience.

How to use a Word of Knowledge

If used correctly, words of knowledge will be a powerful tool in bringing the lost to Christ, as can be seen in the ministry of Jesus. Until you gain more confidence and discernment in knowing when God is speaking to you, my suggestion is for you to operate in humility. If you are ministering to an individual or a group of people and you feel, read, see, think, say, or dream a word of knowledge you don't have to say, "God told me" or "Thus says the Lord."

You can just ask, "is anyone here experiencing this?" or "have you been going through this or that?"

Be open to feedback. It will help you sharpen your gift. If someone confirms that what you said is true, then rejoice and minister in love. If someone denies that what you said is true, then apologize and let the person know you are grateful for their honesty and that you are still learning and growing in your ability to hear God. Don't get discouraged if you get some wrong. You will get better after each attempt.

Also, don't be surprised if someone denies something you said but you still feel a strong impression that it's true. I have had times where I have spoken something to someone and they've literally told me I was wrong. Then minutes, hours or days later they come back confessing it was true but they were ashamed to confess it or were in denial.

As you improve your ability to receive from God, more people will be impacted and drawn to Christ. God wants to use you, so "be strong and courageous" (Joshua 1:9).

Discernment of Spirits and Evangelism

⁸ For to one is given... the distinguishing of spirits (1 Corinthians 12:8, 10)

Closely related to the gift of the word of knowledge is the gift of the discernment of spirits. Although these two gifts are similar and can work together, there are some differences. Nonetheless, the gift of the discernment, or distinguishing of spirits is a very valuable gift when ministering to the lost, especially in the area of deliverance.

What is the Gift of the Discernment of Spirits?

First of all, it is important to realize that this gift is not the gift of "discernment" but "the discernment of spirits." The word "discernment" in the Greek is "diakrisis."[31] It has to do with the act of judging, of coming to a conclusion, and being able to distinguish between two things that seem to be similar. In Scripture, discernment is something every person is capable of doing. We are called as Christians to discern between good and evil, true and false. We develop this ability by using the word of God to gain wisdom and understanding. This discernment has to do with morality or what is manifested in the natural.

But the gift of the discernment of spirits has to do with the supernatural or spiritual realm. When we attach the words "of spirits" to *diakrisis* it becomes the discernment

---

[31] Strong's #1253

of spirits. This gift has to do with being able to judge, come to the conclusion of, or distinguish between spiritual persons either from the kingdom of Satan or the kingdom of God. To be more specific, this gift is the ability to know the name or nature of the spirit(s) working in a person or environment through one or more of our spiritual senses. And because it is a "gift," this is not a natural ability that we can develop naturally but a supernatural grace given to us by the Holy Spirit.

The Gift of the Discernment of Spirits in the Bible

We are not to go around blaming the devil for everything. There are many natural and physical explanations for the things we experience. But in the Bible we can see that many times the causes for certain sicknesses or weaknesses were evil spirits. This gift helps us to determine when this can be the case.

Through the gift of the discernment of spirits Jesus was able to tell when the devil was behind a particular problem. For example, in Luke 13 Jesus healed a woman who suffered for 18 years from an extremely curved spine and said, "And this woman, a daughter of Abraham as she is, whom Satan has bound for eighteen long years, should she not have been released from this bond on the Sabbath day?" (v16). In other words, Jesus recognized Satan was responsible for this woman's sickness and not some natural cause.

It was through this same gift that Paul was able to determine the source and the name of the spirit that was working in a young girl who was accurately prophesying "These men are bond-servants of the Most High God, who are proclaiming to you the way of salvation." [18] She continued doing this for many days. But Paul was greatly annoyed, and turned and said to the spirit, "I command you in the name of Jesus Christ to come out of her!" And it came out at that very moment" (Acts 16:17-18).

This girl had a spirit of divination. She made a true prediction about Paul by the power of a demon. In the natural, this girl would have been seen as a servant of God. She might have even been given a part in one of our churches. But Paul was able to discern, not only the source, but even the name of who was prophesying through her. This was not the Spirit of God, this was the spirit of "Python"[32] (16:16).

The Gift of Discernment of Spirits and Evangelism

This gift can be very valuable when we are ministering or evangelizing the lost. This gift is especially useful when ministering healing or deliverance. There are times when we might pray for someone to be healed and nothing happens. Sometimes the reason is that there is a spirit behind the sickness. We can pray until our face changes colors but nothing will happen until that spirit is cast out of the person. Once the spirit is out of the body the person will be healed automatically or with less effort.

There might be occasions when you must expel a demon from a person, not because of some sickness, but because of some other form of torment, affliction, oppression, bondage, or curse. Through the gift of the discernment of spirits God can show you what spirit is working in the person and thus deliver the person more effectively. Many times God will even give you a word of knowledge to show

---

[32] Strong's #4436

you how and when that spirit entered the person's life. If this is the case you can have the person confess, repent, renounce and close whatever doors gave the enemy access to their lives.

Healing and deliverance are not the only areas where this gift can be useful in reaching the lost. It can play a key role in our prayers and intercession. There are places where certain demonic strongholds and principalities must be dealt with before we can see the fruit of our evangelistic efforts. Knowing who or what we are fighting against will allow us to be more assertive and "box in such a way, as not beating the air" (1 Corinthians 9:26).

How Does This Gift Operate?

As I mentioned before, this gift is the ability to know the name or nature of the spirit(s) working in a person or environment through one or more of our spiritual senses. In the same way that our physical body has senses that allow it to interact with the physical world (sight, hearing, touch, taste, smell), our spirits also have senses.

For example, Paul prays that God would open up the eyes of the heart in Ephesians 1:18. Obviously he is not speaking of the cardiovascular muscle that pumps blood in our body. He is referring to the eyes of the inner man.

When Elisha was surrounded by an army of Arameans in 2 Kings 6, his servant was afraid. Elisha told his servant, "'Do not fear, for those who are with us are more than those who are with them.'[17] Then Elisha prayed and said, 'O Lord, I pray, open his eyes that he may see.' And the Lord opened the servant's eyes and he saw; and behold, the mountain was full of horses and chariots of fire all around Elisha" (v16-17).

The Bible also speaks of our other spiritual senses. Through our spiritual ears we are able to hear the voice of Jesus or the Spirit (John 10:27; Romans 8:16). We are also able to spiritually taste (Psalm 19:10; 1 Peter. 2:2; Hebrews. 5:14) and smell (2 Corinthians 2:15). Our spirits also have a mind (1 Corinthians 2:11) and a will (Matthew 26:41).

So the gift of the discernment of spirits works together with our spiritual senses to determine who or what is operating in a person or environment. Some people with this gift report that when there is a demonic presence they can smell burning sulfur. But when there are angels they smell flowers or something sweet. Others can literally see into the spiritual world and know what is going on. Others have a certain taste come into their mouths. Yet others can feel oppression when it's something demonic or God's peace, joy, or love when it's something heavenly.

This gift is very powerful when ministering healing or deliverance or just praying for the lost. Pray that God would open up your spiritual senses and allow you to operate in the gift of the discernment of spirits.

Prophecy and Evangelism

⁸For to one is given the word of wisdom through the Spirit, and … ¹⁰ to another prophecy (1 Cor. 12:8, 10)

The gifts of the Spirit are normally classified into three categories: revelation gifts, power gifts, and vocal gifts. The gifts of the word of wisdom, word of knowledge, and discernment of spirits are considered revelation gifts because they involve God revealing information or things that could not be known through natural means. The gifts of faith, healing, and working of miracles are considered power gifts because they demonstrate God's supernatural power over nature and the physical dimension.

The gift of prophecy is considered a vocal gift along with the gifts of tongues and interpretation of tongues because they involve speaking something that is being given or revealed by the Holy Spirit. Of all the gifts, this gift of prophecy is one that Paul says we should especially desire (1 Corinthians 14:1, 39) because it edifies the church (14:4), is greater than speaking in tongues (14:5), and is something that we can all do (14:31).

What is the Gift of Prophecy?

In a very specific sense I would define the gift of prophecy as the divine ability to predict the future by revelation and motivation of the Holy Spirit. In other words, it involves the Holy Spirit revealing and motivating a person to speak what is to come. For example the prophet Agabus prophesied (predicted) that there would be a famine in the Roman Empire (Acts 11:27-29) and even that Paul would be persecuted in Jerusalem (Acts 21:10-11). Both predictions came true.

But, in a general sense prophecy also includes revealing the Father's heart. It involves proclaiming or declaring the intent or desire of God for a person, group, nation or situation.

In its most basic form prophecy is hearing what God is saying and passing it forward. When a person is given a message by revelation of the Holy Spirit and then motivated by Him to share that message, that person is prophesying.

Now let me be clear about something. Preaching a sermon is not prophecy, but prophecy can show up in a sermon. A sermon is done by exegeting, meditating on, and analyzing texts, and also by organizing points and illustrations. This process is of course spiritual and its proclamation should be done under the guidance and power of the Spirit. But preaching is not prophecy.

Nonetheless, it is possible to preach a prophetic sermon, sing a prophetic song, write a prophetic poem or paint a prophetic picture.[33] But a prophetic sermon, song, poem, or picture would involve a person receiving (not by natural discernment or interpretation) a message supernaturally from the Holy Spirit and then being motivated by Him to give it.

The Difference between Prophet, Prophecy, and Prophesy

---

[33] Just look at all the prophetic portions of scripture that are filled with poetry, songs, parables, stories, and illustrations with lives of the prophets themselves.

Now, allow me to define or explain the following terms:

Prophet – According to Ephesians 4:11, a New Testament Prophet is a person fulfilling one of the five ministry positions that Christ gave as a gift to the church.[34]

Prophecy – Is the message that is revealed and given by the Holy Spirit.

Prophesy – Is the action of speaking or proclaiming the message that is given and revealed by the Holy Spirit.

The reason it is important to understand the difference between these terms is because many believe that only prophets can receive prophecy and prophesy, but that is not the case. Not everyone is called to be a prophet but every believer can receive a prophecy and prophesy. For example, Acts 21:9 says that Philip the Evangelist had four daughters who "prophesied," not who were "prophets."

In the same way that you can teach without having to be a teacher and you can evangelize without having to be an evangelist, you can prophesy without having to be a prophet. Every believer has the potential to prophesy because every believer has the Holy Spirit and has the ability to hear God.

On the other hand, the ability to hear God doesn't negate the need for the gift of prophecy. Some say, "if we can hear God for ourselves, then why do we need prophets or people to prophesy?" The Bible says that we have no need for a teacher because we have an anointing that

---

[34] If you are interested in learning more about the function and role of a prophet please read *Basic Training for Prophetic Ministry* by Kris Vallotton.

teaches us all things (1 John 2:27), yet there exists the ministry of teacher and the gift of teaching. The gift of prophecy exists for the purpose of confirming and giving further certainty about things that God has already spoken. The gift of prophecy exists for the purpose of helping others who are growing in their ability to hear God. The gift of prophecy exists for the purpose of serving, loving, encouraging, exhorting, and comforting others.[35]

Prophecy and Evangelism

Some may be wondering, "what does the gift of prophecy have to do with evangelism? Isn't this gift only for the church?" The answer to that is "no." Paul says, "[24] But if all prophesy, and an unbeliever or an ungifted man enters, he is convicted by all, he is called to account by all; [25] the secrets of his heart are disclosed; and so he will fall on his face and worship God, declaring that God is certainly among you" (1 Corinthians 14:24-25). Although in this context, an unbeliever is entering a place where God's people are congregating, the point I am trying to make with this passage is that even unbelievers can be touched and impacted for Christ through the gift of prophecy.[36]

---

[35] There are others who believe that if we have the completed written word of God, which is for all people at all times, then there is no need for the gift of prophecy. The problems with this argumentation are the following: (1) These gifts were given by God and they will continue being needed in the Body of Christ until Christ returns (1 Cor. 13:9-10). (2) Though I believe in the Bible being inspired and authoritative, it does not tell me the specific will of God for every area or situation in my life. It might give me general principles but it might not always be specific enough. For example, it does not tell me if I should move my whole family to Africa today, or if I should take this job or that one.

[36] An interesting short book on this topic is *Prophetic Evangelism Made Simple* by Matthew Robert Payne.

If you are evangelizing in the street, or are at work or at home and you prophesy to an unbeliever, that person could "fall on his face and worship God!" Just imagine the impact of someone walking up to you, and by the Spirit of God, they reveal "the secrets" of your heart and give you godly instructions and predictions of what God wants to do and will do in your life. If those predictions come true, neither you nor that unbeliever will ever forget or doubt that there is a God.

How Can I Prophesy?

In reality, the ability to prophesy depends on your ability to hear God and discern what He is saying to you for someone else. Remember, if you are born again and the Holy Spirit lives in you, then you can hear God. If you have been baptized in the Holy Spirit, then the gift of prophecy is in you because of Him. All you need to do is access it by faith. You access it by believing that if you ask Him to give you a message for someone else He is not going to deceive you, lie to you, or give you misinformation or something demonic. If you ask you will receive (Luke 11:9-10). If you ask for bread He won't give you a stone (Luke 11:11-13).

So you can ask the Holy Spirit to give you a message for a person. Then trust that what is revealed to your spirit and shows up in your mind, either by spontaneous words, impressions, thoughts, or images is actually from Him. Remember, of course, to test the word first before giving it. Take it through a filter: Does this contradict God's word or will for the person's life? Will it be edifying?

God may give you certain clues when He wants to use you to give a prophetic word. You may feel an anointing come upon you to speak, you might feel drawn to a certain person or group, you might actually receive a message beforehand, there might be some type of aura or something that sets a person apart, or sometimes there might be a strong sense of compassion towards someone God wants to speak to.

Usually a prophetic word may include words of wisdom[37] and/or words of knowledge. Prophecy can look like a mother holding on to the hands of two children who are fraternal twins. For example, in the book of Revelation John receives seven prophetic messages for seven different churches.

To the church of Smyrna Jesus said, "'I know your tribulation and your poverty (but you are rich), and the blasphemy by those who say they are Jews and are not, but are a synagogue of Satan" (2:9). This part of the prophetic message is a word of knowledge. It was something that was currently true about this church and their situation.

He then continues and says, "Do not fear what you are about to suffer. Behold, the devil is about to cast some of you into prison, so that you will be tested, and you will have tribulation for ten days" (2:10). This portion is purely prophecy in the sense that it is a prediction of something that was going to happen to them in the future.

And the message concludes with a word of wisdom, "Be faithful until death, and I will give you the crown of

---

[37] A word of wisdom is a message of direction or instruction from the Holy Spirit for a particular person or situation. It's a revelation of how to do something or of what to do next.

life" (2:10c). It was a message of instruction, a message of what they were to do in their specific situation.

Practice Makes Perfect

Accuracy in our prophetic words are important and we should not invent words for people. But we should not allow the fear of making a mistake keep us from trying to operate in this gift. Under the old covenant, a person would be considered a false prophet if something he said wasn't true (Deuteronomy 18). But under the new covenant, even Spirit-filled believers might get some details wrong without being considered a false prophet.

Agabus was considered a true Prophet by the church, but he got some details wrong when prophesying over Paul. Kris Vallotton explains,

> He messed up on a few details when he prophesied that the Jews in Jerusalem would bind Paul and hand him over to the Gentiles (Acts 21:10-11)… What actually happened was that the Gentiles rescued Paul from the Jews. Later on in the Book of Acts, the commander turned Paul over to the Jews. This is the opposite of what Agabus prophesied. (Acts 21:32-33)… It is obvious that Agabus was correct about the heart of what God was saying, but he got the details slightly mixed up.[38]

---

[38] *Basic Training for the Prophetic Ministry*, 67. Kindle Edition.

This is just to illustrate that we should not consider someone a false *prophet* because something they said wasn't partially or completely true.[39] We should consider their *prophecy* to be inaccurate. Paul says, "[20] do not despise prophetic utterances. [21] But examine everything *carefully*; hold fast to that which is good" (1 Thessalonians 5:20-21).

This can happen because under the new covenant we don't normally receive prophetic words through some audible voice or open vision. We perceive or discern the internal voice of God. That is why the better we get at hearing God, the more certain we will be at giving prophetic words. The more we practice giving prophetic messages, the better we will get at discerning what is coming from God. The more we get into God's word, spend time in prayer, and feed our spirits, the easier it will get to remain sensitive to the Spirit of God.

Practice with friends. Practice with mature believers who will help you get better, believers who will correct and encourage you in love if what you said is inaccurate. But practice, practice, practice. You will get better. You will grow in this gift. You will impact souls and win sinners for Christ. I know you can do it because Christ is in you, and His Spirit will help you.

---

[39] According to the New Testament a false prophet is a false brother (Matthew 7:15-23). It is an unbeliever, a person who is either deceived or going around deceiving. So when you call someone who truly is a believer, who truly is Spirit-filled; who is just trying to encourage someone else through a prophetic word a false prophet, you are actually speaking condemnation over the person and falsely judging them. If the person is a sincere brother who was wrong, you should correct them in love so that they can get better at hearing God and speaking for Him.

If we want to fish for men, we must use every tool, strategy and weapon given to us by God. And the gift of prophecy is one of those very effective tools.

Miracles and Evangelism

... and to another the effecting of miracles (1 Corinthians 12:10)

We need the supernatural to be a part of our work for God. The Bible says, "For the kingdom of God does not consist in words but in power" (1 Corinthians 4:20). If this statement is true then why is there so much more emphasis on our words than our power when we are being taught to evangelize? Don't get me wrong, we must know what to say and how to say it, for "the gospel is the power of God for those who believe" (Romans 1:16). But we should not be taught words at the exclusion of power.

It was very clear in the mind of Paul that the reason for his effectiveness in ministry was the power of God. It was not about how much knowledge he had (though knowledge is important). It was not about how persuasive or eloquent he was (though we should desire to be persuasive). Adrian Rogers used to say, "Whatever someone can argue me into, someone else can argue me out of." Paul understood that nice sermons, debates or apologetics weren't enough to really draw people into the kingdom. When speaking to the church in Corinth he said,

> And when I came to you, brethren, I did not come with superiority of speech or of wisdom, proclaiming to you the testimony of God. [2] For I determined to know nothing among you except Jesus Christ, and Him crucified. [3] I was with you in weakness and in

fear and in much trembling, [4] and my message and my preaching were not in persuasive words of wisdom, but in demonstration of the Spirit and of power, [5] so that your faith would not rest on the wisdom of men, but on the power of God. (1 Corinthians 2:1-5)

Can you see why we need the supernatural power of God? Can you see why we need the demonstration of the Spirit? It is so that men's faith will not rest on our wisdom, but on God's power! Adrian Rogers would also say, "A man with an experience is never at the mercy of a man with an argument." We must *preach* Christ and Him crucified. Then we must *demonstrate* Christ and Him risen!

So, how do we "demonstrate" Christ? By doing the same miraculous works that He did, and even greater! (John 14:12).[40] This is done through the anointing of the Holy Spirit and the manifestation of spiritual gifts. One of those powerful gifts is the working of miracles.

---

[40] There are many who would argue that "the works that Jesus was referring to in this verse are not miracles. For who could do greater miracles than healing the sick, raising the dead, and walking on water?" They argue that the "greater works" in this verse is referring to the number of souls we would reach. They believe this has to do with "quantity" not "quality." The problem with this argument is that it ignores the context. Jesus challenges his disciples by saying "[10] Do you not believe that I am in the Father, and the Father is in Me? The words that I say to you I do not speak on My own initiative, but the Father abiding in Me does His works. [11] Believe Me that I am in the Father and the Father is in Me; otherwise believe because of the works themselves" (John 14:10-11). Clearly, the works He is referring to are His supernatural deeds! Some examples of those "greater works" His disciples would accomplish are His disciples healing with their shadows (Acts 5:15-16), being transported by the Spirit (Acts 8:39), and handkerchiefs causing healing and deliverance (Acts 19:11-12).

What is a Miracle?

The word miracle is actually the plural form of the Greek word "dunamis."[41] A miracle is something that is done through creative power or ability. A miracle is something that is done or occurs when the natural laws of this world are suspended, manipulated or broken supernaturally.[42] For example, when Jesus walked on water (Matthew 14:22-36; Mark 6:45-56; John 6:16-24) He did something that was impossible to do naturally. The law of gravity would demand that He sink, or at most float on the water, but not walk on it!

Another miraculous work was when Jesus fed the multitude of five thousand men (not including women and children) with five loaves of bread and two fishes (Matthew 14:13-21; Mark 6:30-44; Luke 9:10-17; John 6:1-15). The bread and fish multiplied as they were handed out to each person. At the end of it all the disciples were able to pick up twelve baskets of leftover food!

In both of these examples the natural laws of this world were either suspended manipulated or broken supernaturally.[43] When something like this occurs it is called a miracle.

---

[41] Strong's #1411

[42] This definition is important because there are many who say miracles do not happen at all or happen rarely because if they were common then they wouldn't be miracles. This completely misses the point. It's not a miracle because it's rare. It's a miracle because it isn't natural! Jesus and the disciples did many miracles. Doesn't that nullify that argument?

[43] A miracle is different to a healing. In a healing a person's health is restored or renewed either gradually or immediately. Miracles can be connected to the human body, for example someone rising from the dead or a new arm

The Purpose of Miracles

Miracles are important for many reasons. First and foremost, similar to healing, miracles demonstrate the compassion of a loving God. In Matthew 14, right before Jesus heals the sick and feeds the multitude that gathered, verse 14 says, "When He went ashore, He saw a large crowd, and felt compassion for them..." Every kind act of God is rooted in His good and loving nature. His kindness leads us to repentance (Romans 2:4).

The second purpose of miracles in scripture is to confirm both the identity of Jesus and His relationship to the Father. "Believe Me that I am in the Father and the Father is in Me; otherwise believe because of the works themselves" (John 14:11).

The third purpose of miracles is to confirm both the ministry of believers and the message of the gospel. "And they went out and preached everywhere, while the Lord worked with them, and confirmed the word by the signs that followed" (Mark 16:20; also see Acts 14:3; Hebrews 2:4; 2 Corinthians 12:12).

The fourth purpose of miracles is to attract praise and glory to God.[44] "Immediately he regained his sight and *began* following Him, glorifying God; and when all the people saw it, they gave praise to God" (Luke 18:43). "As soon as He was approaching, near the descent of the Mount of Olives, the whole crowd of the disciples began to praise

---

being created. But miracles do not always have to be connected to the human body.

[44] We should not seek to do miracles so that we can gain fame, popularity, influence or money. Everything we do, whether in word or deed, should be done to glorify God (Colossians 3:17).

God joyfully with a loud voice for all the miracles which they had seen" (Luke 19:37; see also Acts 3:8-11; 4:21-22).

The fifth purpose of miracles is to increase the faith of those who hear the message of the gospel for salvation (1 Corinthians 2:4-5).

> [6] The crowds with one accord were giving attention to what was said by Philip, as they heard and saw the signs which he was performing. [7] For in the case of many who had unclean spirits, they were coming out of them shouting with a loud voice; and many who had been paralyzed and lame were healed. [8] So there was much rejoicing in that city...[12] But when they believed Philip preaching the good news about the kingdom of God and the name of Jesus Christ, they were being baptized, men and women alike. [13] Even Simon himself believed; and after being baptized, he continued on with Philip, and as he observed signs and great miracles taking place, he was constantly amazed. (Acts 8:6-8, 12-13)

Lastly, another purpose for miracles is to build up believers, as can be seen from the context of 1 Corinthians 12 to 14.

How to Operate in Miracles

I believe that there is no secret key to seeing miracles happen. It is my opinion that childlike faith is the first important key to begin seeing miracles. Just like any other gift, faith opens the door to see the supernatural. It is no wonder the gift of faith and the working of miracles are in the same category of power gifts.

But a second important key to see miracles is obedience. I remember Randy Clark mentioning the connection between miracles and obedience in the gospel of John. There are seven miracles recorded in this book, and in almost every instance obedience to Jesus' instructions were necessary. The water would be turned into wine by Jesus but the attendants first had to fill up water jars with water and serve it. The bread and fish were going to be multiplied but first the people had to be organized in groups of 50 and 100 and the disciples needed to serve them in faith. Peter would get to walk on water but first he had to step out of the boat in obedience to Jesus' instructions to come. Lazarus would be raised from the dead but Martha had to have faith and the people had to remove the stone that covered the tomb.

It is interesting that Jesus often said "Truly, truly, I say to you, the Son can do nothing of Himself, unless *it is* something He sees the Father doing; for whatever the Father does, these things the Son also does in like manner" (John 5:19; see also John 5:30; 6:38; 8:28). In other words, Jesus moved in complete obedience and in harmony with the Father's will. And if we walk in faith and obedience to the Father's will we will also see many miracles occur through our hands.

Lastly, I believe intimacy with Christ is the last key. A life surrendered to the presence of Christ will produce the fruit of the miracles. Jesus said in John 15:5 "I am the vine, you are the branches; he who abides in Me and I in him, he bears much fruit, for apart from Me you can do nothing."

In this context "abide" is referring to remaining, staying connected to, and persevering. And so if Christ abides in you and you in Him you will produce His fruit. The fruit of John 15 is not just the fruit of His character, like what is seen in the fruit of the Spirit.[45] It is the fruit of His life, the whole life of Christ. This fruit includes His miraculous works. The life (Spirit) which is in the vine (Christ) passes through and nourishes the branch (you) and will cause the branch to produce fruit consistent to its source. By a life of surrender in intimacy with Christ you will produce His character and His power. Learn to abide and the fruit will be a natural, effortless result.

Miracles have a way of turning heads and opening ears to the message of the gospel. It is one more of the many tools that God has given us to reach the lost. Believe and obey and nothing will be impossible for you (Matthew 17:20).

---

[45] Galatians 5:22-23.

Tongues and Evangelism

With all prayer and petition pray at all times in the Spirit... (Ephesians 6:18)

You might be thinking, "What role can tongues play in evangelizing the lost with power?" This might be the gift of the Spirit that has caused more controversy than any of the others. But when understood and used properly, I believe we will see that this gift is both versatile and very effective in winning the lost for Christ.

What is the Gift of Tongues?

Plain and simple, the gift of tongues is the grace to speak unknown languages – heavenly or earthly. If it's a language that was learned through natural means then it is not the gift of tongues. It must be a language given by the Spirit of God to a Christian.

Now, there are three types of tongues or manifestations of this gift: Preaching tongues, Prophetic tongues, and Prayer tongues. These manifestations or types of tongues are either for public or private use. It is when these distinctions are not understood that conflict arises in its application.

Preaching Tongues

Preaching tongues are earthly tongues. These are languages that are spoken and known here on the earth – English, Spanish, French, German, Chinese, Korean, etc. When this type of tongue is spoken the person is speaking a language that can be understood by people who speak that language. This is the form of tongues that manifested on the day of Pentecost.

> When the day of Pentecost had come, they were all together in one place. ² And suddenly there came from heaven a noise like a violent rushing wind, and it filled the whole house where they were sitting. ³ And there appeared to them tongues as of fire distributing themselves, and they rested on each one of them. ⁴ And they were all filled with the Holy Spirit and began to speak with other tongues, as the Spirit was giving them utterance.

> ⁵ Now there were Jews living in Jerusalem, devout men from every nation under heaven. ⁶ And when this sound occurred, the crowd came together, and were bewildered because each one of them was hearing them speak in his own language. ⁷ They were amazed and astonished, saying, "Why, are not all these who are speaking Galileans? ⁸ And how is it that we each hear *them* in our own language to which we were born? ⁹ Parthians and Medes and Elamites, and residents of Mesopotamia, Judea and Cappadocia, Pontus and Asia, ¹⁰ Phrygia and Pamphylia, Egypt and the districts of Libya around Cyrene, and visitors from Rome, both Jews and proselytes, ¹¹ Cretans and Arabs—we hear them in our *own* tongues speaking of the mighty deeds of God." ¹² And they all continued in amazement and great perplexity, saying to one another, "What does this mean?" ¹³ But others

were mocking and saying, "They are full of sweet wine." (Acts 2:1-13)

These tongues serve as a sign to unbelievers that there is a supernatural God. Paul says, "So then tongues are for a sign, not to those who believe but to unbelievers" (1 Corinthians 14:22a). The reason I call these "Preaching tongues" is because when these tongues are spoken a proclamation of the gospel or of praise takes place as can be seen in the example above. It says in verse 11 "we hear them in our *own* tongues speaking of the mighty deeds of God."

So if you begin to speak an earthly language, by the Spirit of God, you are using the gift of tongues for preaching to the lost. This manifestation serves as a sign to them to help them put their trust in God.

Prophetic Tongues

Prophetic tongues is similar to Preaching tongues in that its purpose is for public use. The distinction lies in how they operate. With Prophetic tongues a person is speaking, not an unknown earthly language, but an unknown heavenly or spiritual language. Within this heavenly language is a message for a person or a group of people. These tongues must operate in unison with the gift of interpretation of tongues for the message to be delivered and understood.

Similar to the gift of prophecy, these tongues are given to be used publicly to edify others. This occurs when the prophetic message is decoded through the gift of interpretation of tongues. Paul says, "[5] Now I wish that you all spoke in tongues, but *even* more that you would prophesy; and greater is one who prophesies than one who speaks in tongues, unless he interprets, so that the church may receive edifying" (1 Corinthians 14:5). In other words, people are edified by this unknown heavenly language when they are able to understand its meaning and message.

So these tongues are useful in evangelism when they are partnered with the interpretation of tongues. You might be praying for a person, and then begin to speak in these tongues. After interpreting them, you are able to bless the person with the prophetic message that was contained in the tongues from God to them.

Praying Tongues

These tongues are a heavenly language that is given to the believer for the purpose of personal edification and private communication with God. "For one who speaks in a tongue does not speak to men but to God... One who speaks in a tongue edifies himself" (1 Corinthians 14:2a, 4a). With these tongues a person can talk to God, sing to God and praise God (1 Corinthians 14:14-15). With these tongues a person can speak mysteries (14:2), make inter-cession (Romans 8:26-27), or even fight spiritual battles (Ephesians 6:18).

These tongues are powerful for evangelism because through them you can intercede for souls and do spiritual warfare on their behalf. And at the same time you are pray-ing for them by the Spirit, you are also strengthening your spirit and causing your inner man to be more sensitive to the spiritual world. Just like there are gateway drugs out there, I believe the gift of tongues is a "gateway gift." This gift opens up the door to many or all of the gifts of the Spirit if practiced properly and often.

For example, Paul says that when we speak in tongues we speak "mysteries by the Spirit" (1 Corinthians 14:2). The meaning being that we speak things that are not understandable by human will or intellect. But what if we could understand what was being said? Then we would receive revelation and edification. And so I believe that when we speak in tongues God is often revealing secrets of the kingdom, words of knowledge, or prophecies of the future. Through interpreting those tongues, I have on many occasions received revelations from God. And through this information I have received creative ideas for sermons, programs, ministries or illustrations; or I have received divine solutions for problems, or been warned of dangers, or have received words of knowledge of things going on with other people, or deep understanding of spiritual things. I love to speak in tongues. I am built up every time I do so.

There is so much I can say on the blessing of the gift of tongues, but I will restrict myself to the immediate context of power evangelism.

Clearing up Misunderstandings

Before we continue I believe it is important we clear up some misconceptions. Not understanding these different types or manifestation of tongues has caused much controversy. But now that we have seen the difference between these types of tongues we can lay out some principles.

First, we should not forbid people to speak in tongues (1 Corinthians 14:39). According to Paul, if people want to speak in tongues in a public setting or at church for personal edification, it is permissible as long as they keep it to themselves and do not make any scene or interrupt the flow of what is going on. "But if there is no interpreter, he must keep silent in the church; and let him speak to himself and to God" (1 Corinthians 14:28).

Second, "all things must be done properly and in an orderly manner" (1 Corinthians 14:40). For all my Pentecostal and Charismatic brethren, if you are going to speak in tongues loud enough that everyone can hear you or that it draws the attention of everyone, then make sure there is an interpretation. If you get really excited and no one interprets you must quiet your tongues and speak at a volume that is discernible between you and God.

This also means, that if there is an unbeliever around, the church should refrain from everyone speaking in tongues at once in a loud manner. If it is going to be out loud, "*it should be* by two or at the most three, and *each* in turn, and one must interpret" (14:27).

I have observed that there is a difference when there is an anointing for a prophetic tongue. Usually, the person may begin to speak softly, but then their tone of voice may increase gradually. And there is an authority that also enters when this gift manifests in this way. So if you begin to speak softly, and then a fire, energy, or anointing begins to increase this can be a sign that God wants to speak a message. But if you notice that you are not getting an interpretation, and neither is anyone else, then you should quiet yourself down for "the spirits of prophets are subject to the prophets" (14:32).

If these two principles that Paul lays down are obeyed, then order will be maintained and people will be edified simultaneously. Tongues are a powerful tool in reaching the lost when understood and used properly.

Those who forbid tongues are wrong. Do not confuse ecclesiastical or liturgical order for the order of the Holy Spirit. He knows how to let fire burn powerfully without it getting out of His control. At the same time those who allow chaos in the name of "freedom of the Spirit" are wrong. Confusion and disorder are not the same thing as the freedom of the Spirit.

How to Speak in Tongues?

Just like any other gift of the Spirit, this gift must be received by grace through faith from the Spirit of God. You can't force it and you can't earn it. You just ask in faith and receive by grace.

> [9] So I say to you, ask, and it will be given to you; seek, and you will find; knock, and it will be opened to you. [10] For everyone who asks, receives; and he who seeks, finds; and to him who knocks, it will be opened. [11] Now suppose one of you fathers is asked by his son for a fish; he will not give him a snake instead of a fish, will he? [12] Or *if* he is asked for an egg, he will not give him a scorpion, will he? [13] If you then, being evil, know how to give good gifts to your children, how much more will *your* heavenly Father give the Holy Spirit to those who ask Him? (Luke 11:9-13)[46]

It is God's will according to this passage to give you of His Holy Spirit.

---

[46] Also see the parallel passage in Matthew 7:7-11.

Some practical tips would be to spend time in prayer and also in praising God. I have seen God give this gift in moments like these. The more you become aware of the presence of God and less self-conscious, the greater the anointing will increase over you. You can also have someone lay hands on you and see if you receive this gift through impartation.

Whatever method you use, step out in faith and begin to speak whatever God puts in your heart, mind or spirit. When I received the gift of tongues, I remember that for some time I had been hearing tongues in my head. I thought I was probably remembering someone else's tongues. I would also get like a knot in my throat when I would praise God or get excited in prayer. But I would stop myself from speaking what came to mind or what I felt coming to my mouth until the day I decided to step out in faith. At first I spoke small syllables. But the more I practiced the more this gift developed.

So step out in faith the next time you ask for this gift, or someone prays for you, or you're praising God and feel something rising in your throat. God will not judge you or condemn you for doing this. It is not "demonic" nor "carnal" to do this. Remember His promise in Luke 11.

Father, I pray for an impartation from the Spirit of God for your child. May they receive the gift of tongues. May your anointing begin to come upon them. May fire begin to rise in their belly and bubble up into their throat in Jesus name!

Dreams, Visions and Evangelism

And your young men shall see visions, And your old men shall dream dreams (Acts 2:17)

Dreams and Visions are a phenomena as old as humanity and as common as the cold. Everyone experiences them, but not everyone understands their meaning nor their relevance. Whether you are a believer or not you have experienced at least one sort of vision or the other. In this chapter, I want to give a brief description of the different types of visions and how they relate to evangelism.

What is a Vision?

Before discussing the different types of visions I believe it is important that we first understand what a vision is. A vision is an image or revelation we can see with our spiritual eyes. Remember that we are not just flesh and bone. We are spirits within a body. Our spirits exist in order for us to relate or interact with the spiritual world. "God is spirit, and those who worship Him must worship in *spirit* and truth." (John 4:24; emphasis mine).

Although, with our soul and body we are conscious of the physical world around us, our spirit is conscious of the spiritual world that exists all around us. So one of the ways in which we can receive information from the spiritual world is through visions. God temporarily removes the veil between our soul and spirit. Then He allows our mind (or soul) to see (or have a vision of) images or receive revelation from the spiritual world.

Different Types of Visions

Now, there are four types of visions, four types of ways that God allows us to see or receive revelation from the spiritual world. These types of visions are: Trance visions, Open visions, Mental Visions, and Night Visions (Dreams).

Trance visions are visions that take place when we lose awareness of the physical world around us and move completely into the spiritual world in our minds or bodies.[47] Peter had this form of vision in Acts 10, "[9] On the next day, as they were on their way and approaching the city, Peter went up on the housetop about the sixth hour to pray. [10] But he became hungry and was desiring to eat; but while they were making preparations, he fell into a trance" (v9-10). In other words, Peter lost awareness of his surroundings and was only conscious of the spiritual vision he was seeing.[48]

Open visions are visions that you can see with your eyes open. With these visions, you do not lose consciousness of your physical surrounding. Instead you are able to see both the spiritual and physical world simultaneously. Once again Peter is a great example of this type of vision. In Acts 12, Peter was going to be executed by Herod after the feast of Passover. But in the night time while Peter was sleeping, God sent an angel to rescue him in response to the fervent prayers of the church. The angel woke him up, the chains fell off his feet and wrists and he escorted Peter out of the prison. Verse 9 says, "And he went out and continued

---

[47] See 2 Corinthians 12:1-4 to see this described.

[48] Maria Woodworth Etter was known for having many of these types of visions. She would often go into a trance even when preaching. This experience could last her from a few minutes to a few hours.

to follow, and he did not know that what was being done by the angel was real, but thought he was seeing a vision." In other words, Peter believed he was in another trance, but he was actually seeing all of this take place literally with his eyes wide open. He was seeing a spiritual being moving in the physical realm. The guards could not see any of this, but Peter could because the veil was temporarily brought down so that he could escape with the angel.[49]

The third type of vision is known as a Mental Vision. Both the third and fourth type of visions are more common. These are spiritual things you can see in your mind, or in your imagination. You might have heard the expressions "your mind's eye." In the same part of you that you can see memories or create images, you can also see spiritual entities, information, or revelation. If you remember, this is one of the ways that you receive words of knowledge. This is a common way to see prophetically or discern spirits. These visions can occur with both your eyes closed or your eyes open. You are conscious of the physical world but are seeing in your soul what is going on in the spiritual world.

The final type of vision is a Night Vision. This is more commonly known as a dream. "In a dream, a vision of the night, When sound sleep falls on men, While they slumber in their beds" (Job 33:15). These are visions that occur when a person is asleep. They are no longer conscious of the physical world because their body is in a state of rest. But although their body is resting their soul and spirit are not. In these visions you can receive revelation

---

[49] Another very famous example of an open vision is found in 2 Kings 6 when Elisha prays for the eyes of his servant to be opened and he see's horses and chariots of fire surrounding Elisha.

from God or be visited by spiritual beings – demons, angels, or God Himself.

The Purpose of Dreams and Visions

There are many visions and dreams recorded in the Bible from Genesis to Revelation. Although we cannot go into each of these dreams in detail I believe there are common reasons why they are given. I believe they are given for revelation, instruction, direction, guidance, confirmation, encouragement, and comfort. About dreams for instance, the Word says,

> Indeed God speaks once, Or twice, *yet* no one notices it. [15] In a dream, a vision of the night, When sound sleep falls on men, While they slumber in their beds,[16] Then He opens the ears of men, And seals their instruction, [17] That He may turn man aside *from his* conduct, And keep man from pride; [18] He keeps back his soul from the pit, And his life from passing over into Sheol. (Job 33:14-18)

In other words, there are times that God tries to speak to us and get our attention when we are awake. But because we are so busy with the cares of life, sometimes He has to wait until we are sleeping in order to reach us and instruct us to keep us from sin, or from perishing, or warning us of danger.

Now, more relevant to this book is the fact that God can give us dreams and visions for the purpose of reaching the lost. When Peter had the trance vision in Acts 10, it was to instruct him on reaching out to Gentile believers who would also become part of the family of God and heirs of salvation. The amazing thing, was that the people whom Peter would preach to also had their own vision that opened them up to hear the gospel and change their eternal destiny.

In Acts 16, we find Paul on one of his missionary journeys. He was planning to travel east into Asia, but God had other plans. He did not permit Paul or his companions to travel east, but instead they were instructed to go west, into Macedonia, to preach the gospel. If it were not for that key vision and Paul's obedience and sensitivity to the Spirit, we would be reading about a completely different church in history today.

Dreams and visions are one of the primary reasons that Muslims, Hindus, and Buddhists and people from the third world are turning to Christ. They are not being persuaded so much by our apologetics, our books and our great fancy services or programs. They are encountering God through visions, dreams, healings, deliverances, and miracles!

There is a reason that God promised that together with the pouring out of His Spirit, people – young and old, male and female – would be having dreams and visions. The experience of the supernatural would be made available to everyone regardless of age or gender. God wants a relationship with us. He wants to reach us with every means possible.

We should be in the business of saving souls. One of the powerful means God has chosen to reveal Himself to us and to instruct us personally is through dreams and visions. We should not ignore them or take them lightly. Destinies and people are in the balance.

What Should we do Now?

I believe the first thing we should do, now that we understand these truths, is cultivate a sensitivity to the Spirit. We should spend time with God in prayer, and worship and most importantly, in the Word. It is through the word of God that we will be able to filter out the bad and receive the good.

Next, we should be expecting God to speak to us through dreams and visions. Have a notepad or something to write with or record the dreams you have. Don't always ignore the mental images you receive. Through the Spirit and the word of God discern its origin and its purpose. If God is leading you, obey His instructions. Share the gospel with the lost. Prophesy to others.

I, for example, am so anxious and expecting for God to speak to me in dreams that I sleep with my phone nearby so that I can record audibly whatever dream I remember. Even when I pray, I keep my tablet or computer close so that if I hear or see anything from God I am able to write it down.

Lastly, invest your time and resources in learning about dreams and visions. Read books, hear messages, watch videos, attend conferences that will help you learn how to interpret dreams and visions, and that will help you develop your spiritual senses.

God wants to speak to you every day. He wants to do it through the Scriptures and also by the inner witness of the Spirit. But He also wants to reveal Himself through dreams and visions.

May the Lord give you a spirit of wisdom and revelation in the knowledge of Him. May He open up the eyes of your heart so that you will know what is the hope of His calling, the riches of the glory of His inheritance in the saints, and the surpassing greatness of His power toward you because you believe. That power is in accordance with the working of the strength of His might which He brought about in Christ, when He raised Him from the dead and seated Him at His right hand in the heavenly *places*, far above all rule and authority and power and dominion, and every name that is named, not only in this age but also in the one to come (Ephesians 1:17-21).

Cooperating with Angels in Evangelism

Are they not all ministering spirits, sent out to render service for the sake of those who will inherit salvation? (Hebrews 1:14)

Angels are a fascinating subject. Movies, books, and even television programs have been made about them. They seem to be so near yet so elusive. Nonetheless, the Bible frequently mentions their involvement in the affairs of men. Even more relevant to this book, angels are involved in the preaching and propagation of the gospel. If we could learn to understand who they are and what is their purpose, we could then learn how to encounter and cooperate with them more frequently when evangelizing the lost.

What are angels?

Both in the Hebrew (malak) and the Greek (aggelos) the word "angel" actually means "messenger." So angels are heavenly supernatural messengers. But they are also ministering spirits (Hebrews 1:14). Or better said, they are spirits who serve.

The Bible describes them in many different ways. Some of these ways even denote ranks among them.

- Hosts (1 Samuel 17:45; Psalm 89:8)
- Watchers (Daniel 4:13, 17)
- Sons of the mighty (Psalm 29:1)
- Sons of God (Job 1:6)

- Stars (Revelation 12:4)
- Archangels (Jude 1:9)
- Seraphim (Isaiah 6:2)
- Cherubim (Genesis 3:24)
- Living Creatures (Revelation 4:8)[50]

Angels in the New Testament

Angels can be seen in the New Testament from beginning to end. Timothy Berry says,

> In the New Testament, Gabriel shows up again, appearing to the father of John the Baptist, Zacharias in Luke 1:11-19. Then to Mary the mother of Jesus in Luke 1:26-38 and to Joseph in Matthew 1:20-24. An angel appears to Joseph on two more occasions in dreams in Matthew 2:13 and 2:19. As mentioned before, angels ministered to Jesus in Matthew 4:11, Mark 1:13, and Luke 22:43. As stated in chapter 1, Jesus very likely had more encounters with angels. We conclude this from his statement in John 1:51, about angel's ascending and descending upon him. Angels appeared at the tomb of Jesus' resurrection in Matthew 28:5; Luke 22:43; John 20:12. Two men appeared at the ascension of Jesus in Acts 1:10. An angel rescued the apostles from prison in Acts 5:19 and again Peter in Acts 12:7-10. Paul had an experience with an angel in Acts 27:23, and in 2 Corinthians 12 Paul describes how some of his

---

[50] Rand Clark et al., *Entertaining Angels: Engaging the Unseen Realm*, (Mechanicsburg, PA: Apostolic Network of Global Awakening, 2011), 51-58.

heavenly experiences and visions were so amazing that he could not tell anyone. John had a very long visitation with many angels and Jesus Christ in the book of Revelation. Also, in many of these accounts the angels and individuals had a conversation back and forth, meaning that we as humans can communicate with angels when initiated by them.[51]

Now this is not an exhaustive list of angelic encounters in the New Testament. It is just a general sample that can show how involved angelic beings were in the life of believers from the beginning.

The Purpose of Angels

Now why do angels exist? What is their purpose? I believe the answer to these questions will shed light on how they are relevant to us. Though there are many things that can be said, I will focus on the essential ones.

First and foremost, angels exist to give glory to God. From the beginning to the end of the Bible, angels are seen as surrounding God and worshipping Him day and night. Revelation 4:8 says, "And the four living creatures, each one of them having six wings, are full of eyes around and within; and day and night they do not cease to say, 'Holy, holy, holy is the Lord God, the Almighty, who was and who is and who is to come.'" Revelation 7:11-12 says, "[11] And all the angels were standing around the throne and around the elders and the four living creatures; and they fell on their faces before the throne and worshiped God, [12] saying,

---

[51] Ibid, 37-38.

'Amen, blessing and glory and wisdom and thanksgiving and honor and power and might, be to our God forever and ever. Amen.'"

Many of the testimonies of people or churches who encounter or see angels describe these visitations taking place during a time of exuberant praise and worship. It is almost as if the praise on earth attracts these heavenly beings to participate in giving honor and glory to Him who is worthy. God is enthroned upon the praises of His people (Psalm 22:3). In other words, heaven touches earth when praise and worship is lifted up.

Secondly, angels exist to carry out the will of God. "Bless the Lord, you His angels, Mighty in strength, who perform His word, Obeying the voice of His word! [21] Bless the Lord, all you His hosts, You who serve Him, doing His will" (Psalm 103:20-21). Of course God could do everything on His own, but He allows us and the angels to participate in the joy of His works by carrying out His will.

Thirdly, angels exist to serve the church. Remember, "Are they not all ministering spirits, sent out to render service for the sake of those who will inherit salvation?" (Hebrews 1:14). They are not submitted to us as slaves. They work with us as partners in expanding the will of God and spreading the gospel. Angels can be sent to us to strengthen us (Luke 22:43), deliver us from physical harm or demonic attacks (Psalm 91:11-12; Acts 12:7-10), provide us with God's supernatural provision (1 Kings 19:5-8), give us divine revelation or instructions (Acts 8:26-40; book of Revelation), remove any hindrances for us to preach the gospel (Acts 5:17-21), and even prepare the hearts of unbelievers to receive our preaching of the gospel (Acts 10).

If this is all true, then shouldn't we be more open to angelic encounters and heavenly help?

Some Do's and Don'ts of Cooperating with Angels

If we are to somehow take an active role in having these angelic encounters or cooperating with heaven, there are some really important things we should do and not do.

First we should not worship angels. I know this might seem obvious, but even the most spiritual of us can fall mistakenly into angel worship. The beloved apostle John experienced this in the book of Revelation and the angel himself responded, "Then I fell at his feet to worship him. But he said to me, 'Do not do that; I am a fellow servant of yours and your brethren who hold the testimony of Jesus; worship God. For the testimony of Jesus is the spirit of prophecy'" (19:10).

The very first two commandments of the Decalogue command us not to worship or have any other gods except the real God. We should not become so infatuated with angels that we somehow make them an idol or the object of our worship or prayers.

This brings me to a second suggestion. Do not pray to angels. The Bible says, "For there is one God, *and* one mediator also between God and men, *the* man Christ Jesus" (1 Timothy 2:5). Our prayers should be directed to the Trinitarian Godhead. If we would like to see angels or seek their assistance we should direct our prayers to God. It is not wrong to ask for these experiences. This is exactly what Manoah, the father of Samson, did when wanting to receive instructions on how to raise Samson (see Judges 13).

Third, keep an open mind to the supernatural and visitations of these beings. A person who is skeptical or resistant to such an encounter will probably never experience it or acknowledge it. "Without faith it is impossible to please God" (Hebrews 11:6).

Some people might feel uncomfortable with this. It is totally normal. Many have encountered false angelic appearances throughout history and have gone astray. That's why you should use the principles spoken of in this book to test the spirits and filter out what's bad. Annie Byrne in the book *Entertaining Angels* [52] actually gives some advice to discern if the encounter you have is from God or not. She mentions things like: Does the encounter bring edification, consolation, and exhortation? Is it in agreement with the Bible? Does it exalt Jesus? Does it produce good fruit? Are the predictions accurate? Do the accurate predictions turn people toward God? Does the encounter bring liberty or bondage? Does it bring life or death? Does the Holy Spirit bear witness to its truth?

Fourth, as I mentioned earlier, praise and worship creates an atmosphere that invites the angelic. So in your times of praise and worship, be aware of your surroundings and keep your heart open to whatever God may want to do. There have been times when I have worshipped God and have felt wind passing through my hands or body. The surprising thing is that on certain occasions this has occurred when there wasn't any natural reason for such wind. The air conditioning or fans weren't producing such an effect. There was no draft from open doors or windows. The Bible says, "And of the angels He says, 'Who makes His angels

---

[52] Ibid, 103-104

winds, And His ministers a flame of fire'" (Hebrews 1:7). Experiences like this can possibly be angelic beings making themselves known.

Fifth, live in the perfect will of God. In the scriptures, angels often show up when people are working for God or carrying out their ministry or under spiritual or physical attack for doing the will of God. If you are walking in obedience to the will of God and are involved in doing His work, it is probable that angels will be present to assist you on many occasions, even if you do not notice. For example, the Bible says, "Do not neglect to show hospitality to strangers, for by this some have entertained angels without knowing it" (Hebrews 13:2). Angels are also activated when we declare Gods word.

My final piece of advice, is to also pray for unbelievers to have true encounters with angels that would cause them to open their hearts for the gospel. Just like Cornelius, people can be impacted by such encounters. The Holy Spirit is the one who brings conviction of sin, but angels are our invisible "coworkers" in the ministry.

We Live Under an Open Heaven

I do not remember where I first heard this concept, but it has been such a blessing to me. We live under an open heaven. Which means we have free access to the blessings of heaven and the ability to serve as a door or bridge for that which is heavenly to be manifested here on the earth. Let me explain.

In Genesis 28, Jacob has a dream where he encounters God. In that dream, he sees a ladder that "was set on the earth with its top reaching to heaven; and behold, the angels of God were ascending and descending on it" (28:12). After he sees this ladder and the angels going to and fro between earth and heaven, verse 17 says, "He was afraid and said, 'How awesome is this place! This is none other than the house of God, and this is the gate of heaven.'"

So he noticed there was a portal to heaven in God's house, with a ladder serving as a bridge between this dimension and the next. Angels were moving freely up and down that ladder.

It is interesting to note that Jesus uses this illustration to talk about Himself. After giving a word of knowledge to Nathanael that caused him to place his faith in Jesus, John tells us, "And He said to him, 'Truly, truly, I say to you, you will see the heavens opened and the angels of God ascending and descending on the Son of Man'" (1:51).

The Bible tells us that Jesus is God (John 1:1) and that God decided to "dwell among us" (1:14). The word "dwell" in this verse means to set a tent or tabernacle.[53] We can actually say that God "tabernacled" among us in the person of Christ. Jesus didn't only come and live among men, He was literally God in the flesh. Jesus was "the house of God and the gate of heaven" here on earth. So He served as a mobile access point and bridge that allowed free travel for angels. Angelic activity was constantly around Jesus. Wherever Jesus went, He literally brought heaven to earth.

But now that He has ascended, does any such house exist? Does any such gate exist here on the earth? A place

---

where heaven can invade and angels can descend and ascend? Yes!

The Bible says of each believer that we are temples of the Holy Spirit (1 Corinthians 3:16; 6:19). We are literally God's house here on the earth and God literally dwells in us. Because of this, we are gates, we serve as bridges between heaven and earth. The supernatural should literally be happening everywhere we go. Angels are, moving, ascending, and descending upon our lives. They work to carry praise and intercession up and answers and blessings down.

Everywhere we go, people should be able to have a little heaven from us. Heaven should be able to do its will in our lives because we serve as channels of God's presence and love. We are literally living as "gatekeepers" to the supernatural. We live under a constant open heaven. The only things that block or hinder these encounters or invasions from heaven to occur in our lives are our lack of faith, lack of love and our un-renewed minds. As I have heard Todd White say, "The only 'blocks' to the supernatural is right between our ears."

So I encourage you to cooperate with the angels. As you fulfill the Great Commission, ask God for angelic assistance where ever it is needed. Pray for unbelievers to have these encounters. Be open to the supernatural. Live holy and loving lives. Spread the fragrance of heaven where ever you go. You are literally a house of God and a gate to heaven for the lost here on the earth.

The Gospel and Evangelism

For I am not ashamed of the gospel, for it is the power of God for salvation to everyone who believes… (Romans 1:16)

Although the focus of this book is the power of the Holy Spirit and the supernatural in relation to evangelism, it would not be complete if we did not speak about the message of the gospel. The gospel message itself is supernatural and is even referred to as "the power of God for salvation to everyone who believes" (Romans 1:16). We cannot evangelize completely without proclaiming this message as well as demonstrating it. The signs are to follow those who believe and also the message that is preached.

What is the gospel?

The word "gospel" literally means "good news." The Greek word is "euanggelion"[54] and is used 76 times in the New Testament. This word is used to describe the good news of Jesus with phrases like "the gospel," "the gospel of Jesus Christ," "the gospel of the kingdom," "the gospel of glory," "the gospel of God" or even "my gospel."

Although many have offered varying definitions for the gospel there are a few places in Scripture that actually define the gospel of Jesus Christ. The first is in Romans 1:1-4:

Paul, a bond-servant of Christ Jesus, called *as* an apostle, set apart for the gospel of God,

---

[54] Strong's #2098

> ² which He promised beforehand through His
> prophets in the holy Scriptures, ³ concerning
> His Son, who was born of a descendant of
> David according to the flesh, ⁴ who was de-
> clared the Son of God with power by the res-
> urrection from the dead, according to the
> Spirit of holiness, Jesus Christ our Lord.

The second place in the New Testament that tells us exactly what the gospel message is, is found in 1 Corinthians 15:1-4:

> Now I make known to you, brethren, the gos-
> pel which I preached to you, which also you
> received, in which also you stand, ² by which
> also you are saved, if you hold fast the word
> which I preached to you, unless you believed
> in vain. ³ For I delivered to you as of first im-
> portance what I also received, that Christ died
> for our sins according to the Scriptures, ⁴ and
> that He was buried, and that He was raised on
> the third day according to the Scriptures.

If we were to combine these verses, we would notice they share a couple of things in common. They both speak of Jesus having died and risen back to life. So at the core of the gospel message is the death and resurrection of Jesus. But there are also other details that can be seen. For instance, in the passage in Romans, Paul speaks of Jesus being God's son according to the Spirit and the son of David according to the flesh.

So if I were to define the gospel from just looking at these two verses, I would say **the gospel of Jesus Christ is the good news of who Jesus *is* and *what* He has done.**

This definition would fit perfectly with the fact that the four *Gospels* actually tell us the story of who Jesus *is* and *what* He did for us. Jesus is the gospel.

This message, and this message alone is "the power of God for salvation for those who believe." This is the message that people need to hear to get saved.

The Need to Preach the Gospel

Paul himself understood this when he said, "I determined to know nothing among you except Jesus Christ, and Him crucified" (1 Corinthians 2:2). The message that people needed to hear was "Jesus is the son of God, who became flesh. He lived a sinless life and was anointed by the Holy Spirit and with power and went around doing good and healing all who were oppressed by the devil. He took our sins upon Himself and died on a cross as a substitute to receive God's wrath. But on the third day God raised Him from the dead and now He lives to make intercession and deliver all those who call upon His name for salvation."

Of course we do not need to preach it word for word as I described it. But that should be at the core of what we preach when evangelizing the lost. Many times when we evangelize our focus becomes our testimony or our experience. Our testimony and experience is good because it illustrates God's goodness, but our presentation should definitely include and emphasize who Jesus is and what He has done for us through His death and resurrection.

I have also seen people preaching doctrines and traditions of men when evangelizing. I have seen them condemn and criticize when evangelizing. My brothers and sisters, just preach the gospel! That message has the power to save sinners if people will listen and believe! Stop trying to clean the fish before you catch them!

Of course, preaching the gospel is not a guarantee that sinners will listen, but it is the only message through which they can be saved. If you still feel unsure or nervous about sharing the gospel, there are many websites and books that can help you with how you can proclaim this message. Nonetheless, whatever method you use, make sure the good news of who Jesus is and what He has done is at the center of your message.

Leading Someone to Christ

After you have shared the gospel with someone, what next? Many people have trouble leading others to Christ. There are some churches and traditions that are against altar calls and leading others in a sinner's prayer but I think there's nothing wrong with it as long as we don't use it as some type of magic formula and think people are automatically saved just for repeating some words. So let's take a look at the type of prayer I lead people in and the scriptural basis for such a prayer.

Before I lead someone in the prayer I like to first make sure the person understands the gospel. Then I like to explain what will be expected of them if they choose to become a Christian. Christianity is not about a religion of rules of what you can and cannot do. It is about a relationship with a person that you are making a commitment to follow. I do this because of what Jesus said in Luke 14:25-33 about counting the cost for being His follower. If the person expresses that they are willing to commit their lives to Him, I lead them in the following prayer and I generally[55] ask the person to repeat it with their mouths and from their hearts:

> *Lord Jesus, I come to you today and I admit that I am a sinner and I am guilty and deserve to be punished and go to hell. But I believe that you love me and that you died for my sins on the cross and that you were raised to life on the third day. Today, I choose to surrender my life to you and to turn away from this world. Have mercy on me and save me. I confess you as my Lord and Savior in the name Jesus, amen.[56]*

Each of these sentences are based on Scripture. I don't know how anyone could critique such a prayer. Like I mentioned, we shouldn't treat it as a magic formula. You are not saved for repeating it, you are saved because you believe the gospel and are repenting of your sins and dedicating your life to Jesus. Romans 10:9-10 says, "that if you confess with your mouth Jesus *as* Lord, and believe in your heart that God raised Him from the dead, you will be saved; [10] for with the heart a person believes, resulting in righteousness, and with the mouth he confesses, resulting in salvation."

---

[55] There are some people for instance who are sick or on a death bed and cannot articulate with their mouth their confession, but maybe they can blink their eyes or squeeze your hand. Be led by the Spirit and be sensitive to the person and context you are ministering in.

[56] Passages that this prayer is based on are: Luke 18:13; Romans 6:23; John 3:16; Romans 10:9-10.

So if you share the gospel with someone and you have explained the implications of giving their lives to Jesus, feel free to lead them in a similar prayer. It doesn't have to be just like that. You can even allow them to pray whatever is in their heart as long as they are repenting of their sins and placing their trust in Christ. If they genuinely do this, you can assure them that the Bible says their names have been written in heaven in the Lamb's book of life and that all of heaven is rejoicing as they witnessed this life changing decision.

I would then encourage them to: (1) to read the Bible daily; (2) spend time in prayer daily; (3) find a church rooted in the Bible, the Holy Spirit, and love and to attend it regularly. This is all necessary if they want to grow in Christ and remain faithful.[57]

This isn't complicated, so don't complicate it and don't become intimidated. Just share your experience, share the gospel, and lead the person in prayer. You can do it. I believe in you.

---

[57] If possible, I would also suggest for you to lay hands on them and pray that God would fill them with the Holy Spirit immediately.

Anointed Preaching and Evangelism

The Spirit of the Lord is upon Me, Because He anointed Me to preach the gospel to the poor. (Luke 4:18)

There is much talk in our days about the anointing. But what is it and why is it necessary to have if we are going to reach the lost? I believe preaching without the anointing of God is the reason that much of the sermons and teachings of today have accomplished very little in our congregations and even less in the streets. Nonetheless, God wills us to be anointed so that we may preach this gospel effectively to those who are perishing.

What is the Anointing?

I would like to begin defining the anointing by stating what it is not. The anointing is not emotionalism though it will produce excitement. The anointing is not meanness though it will bring conviction. The anointing is not charisma though it is attractive.

I believe the simplest way to define the anointing is to say that it is the temporary empowering presence and power of the Holy Spirit.[58] Allow me to explain.

---

[58] I say temporary because it is an authority or power that comes when doing something for God but lifts once we're done. This is different to the infilling of the Spirit which is a continual flow of the Spirit as a way of life.

The Greek word for anointing is "chrio."[59] It means to rub or anoint with oil. Both objects and people were anointed in the Old Testament. Something that was anointed was something that was consecrated or separated for special use by God. Mostly prophets, priests and kings were anointed.

Now, the oil with which they were anointed is symbolic of the Holy Spirit. And so, when these men were anointed with oil and consecrated by God, they were divinely empowered by the Holy Spirit to fulfill their roles. The Holy Spirit would come upon them and give them supernatural power or abilities. So we see a Samson who could defeated hundreds of men or lift up city gates when this power came upon him. Or a David who could play the harp and cause demons to lift off of a tormented Saul.

When someone is anointed with Holy Spirit they can do the supernatural. *"You know of* Jesus of Nazareth, how God anointed Him with the Holy Spirit and with power, and *how* He went about doing good and healing all who were oppressed by the devil, for God was with Him" (Acts 10:38).

The Anointing in our Preaching

The reason we need the anointing when preaching the gospel is because it makes all the difference in the world. You can hear two people sing the same song with the same chords and the same melodies. But while the one who sings without the anointing might please the ear, the one who sings with the anointing will reach the heart, bring

---

[59] Strong's #5548

you to tears, cause people to repent of their sins, want more of God and even cause people to be delivered or healed.

The same is true with preaching. Preaching without the anointing does not produce life, does not pierce the heart, does not convict the soul. It might be eloquent, homiletically sound, and even filled with fervor but it will not produce change. This is the type of preaching that has been done for so long and people's lives have not been impacted.

But preaching with the anointing will produce life, pierce the heart, convict the soul, produce change, and impact the people. We can see this with Peter's sermon on the day of Pentecost. After the Holy Spirit came upon him, he went out and spoke to the people. Here is the result of this anointed message:

> Now when they heard *this*, they were pierced to the heart, and said to Peter and the rest of the apostles, "Brethren, what shall we do?" [38] Peter *said* to them, "Repent, and each of you be baptized in the name of Jesus Christ for the forgiveness of your sins; and you will receive the gift of the Holy Spirit. [39] For the promise is for you and your children and for all who are far off, as many as the Lord our God will call to Himself." [40] And with many other words he solemnly testified and kept on exhorting them, saying, "Be saved from this perverse generation!" [41] So then, those who had received his word were baptized; and that day there were added about three thousand souls. [42] They were continually devoting themselves to the apostles' teaching and to

> fellowship, to the breaking of bread and to prayer. (Acts 2:37-42)

The people were "pierced to the heart." They were convicted by the Holy Spirit and converted. Matter of fact they didn't even wait for some altar calling, they asked the preacher what they needed to do to get saved. At the end of that day 3,000 souls were saved and added to the kingdom of God!

The anointing of the Holy Spirit fills the preachers' words with authority and influence. It gives life in the mouth of an earthly preacher to speak the living word of God with power. Anointed preaching will bring a heaviness or a tangibility of the presence of God. Heaven will fill the atmosphere.

Where do we get the Anointing?

Can I be honest with you? I believe in impartation. I believe in studying and rightly dividing the word of truth. But it is my opinion that the anointing comes from time in the secret place. I believe prayer is the answer for power.

I believe that many pulpits are lacking of power because they are lacking of prayer. I believe many preachers are lacking of anointing because they are lacking of prayer. They look for all the dynamic and creative ways to "wow" the audience. They believe that diligent Bible study, good apologetics and the transmitting of information will convince or persuade the people. But they spend very little time on their knees seeking the presence and power of the Holy Spirit for their preaching.

I once read somewhere, "Before we can speak to men about God, we must first learn to speak to God about men." E. M. Bound says,

> What the church needs today is not more machinery or better, not new organizations or more and novel methods, but men whom the Holy Spirit can use – men of prayer, men mighty in prayer. The Holy Spirit does not flow through methods, but through men. He does not come on machinery, but on men. He does not anoint plans, but men – men of prayer...
>
> The sermon is made in the closet. The man – God's man – is made in the closet. His life and his profoundest convictions were born in his secret communion with God. The burdened and tearful agony of his spirit, his weightiest and sweetest messages were received when alone with God. Prayer makes the man: prayer makes the preacher; prayer makes the pastor. The pulpit of this day is weak in praying. The pride of learning is against the dependent humility of prayer. Prayer is with the pulpit too often only official – a performance of the routine of service. Prayer is not to the modern pulpit the mighty force it was in Paul's life or Paul's ministry. Every preacher who does not make prayer a mighty factor in his own life and ministry is weak as a fascinator in God's work and is

> powerless to project God's cause in the world.[60]

Praying Christians is the need of the hour. This is the hardest but sweetest way of receiving the anointing to preach.

Will it take time? Yes. But will the results be worth it? Yes. F. B. Meyer once said, "If Christ waited to be anointed before He went to preach, no young man ought to preach until he, too, has, been anointed by the Holy Ghost."[61] When we see powerful outpourings of the Holy Spirit, strong conviction upon sinners and mighty repentance in people's lives we will give thanks to God for the anointing and the time we spend with Him in secret, where no one else sees. In that closet there is no applause or praise from men, but there will be from God. The results of that time will be seen publicly when preaching the beautiful gospel of Jesus Christ.

---

[60] "Power Through Prayer," in *The Complete Works of E. M. Bounds on Prayer*, (Grand Rapids, MI: Baker Books, 2004) 447, 449.

[61] Leonard Ravenhill, *Why Revival Tarries* (Minneapolis, MN: Bethany House, 1987), 56.

Prayer and Evangelism

Brethren, my heart's desire and my prayer to God for them is for their salvation (Romans 10:1)

How much time do you spend in prayer? How important do you believe prayer is in connection to winning souls? Even though I have spoken briefly on prayer and will mention it again in the next chapter, I believe it is worth emphasizing. I believe in the power of prayer.

Souls Need to be "Birthed" through Prayer

There is a man who has visited my congregation on various occasions who frequently reminded me, "souls need to be birthed at the altar." What he meant is that we need to pray for souls until they are birthed into the kingdom through our prayers. We must intercede, we must travail in agony for the souls of men until they are delivered from the kingdom of darkness and brought into the liberty of the sons of God. In the natural, do not women travail with birth pangs until the child is brought into this world? The same is true in the spiritual. We must persevere in prayer if we want to see more sinners converted.

The art of travailing for souls has been lost in many churches. But the need to travail, to agonize in prayer for the souls of men is Biblical. Isaiah said "As soon as Zion travailed, she also brought forth her sons" (66:8). Paul travailed for the souls of the Galatian church, "My children, with whom I am again in labor until Christ is formed in you" (Galatians 4:19). They had been birthed through prayer, and after some time were "bewitched" or corrupted by false doctrine. And so he went back to praying for them until Christ was formed in them once again.

The art of travailing in prayer is the art of suffering pain in your soul because of the lost men and women. It is to pray with tears as you realize that men and women are sinking into hell rapidly and the only hope they have is Christ reaching down with infinite mercy to deliver them from death. To travail in prayer is to take the place of an intercessor who has felt what God feels towards a sinner and to pray with His heart, with His passion, and with His words.

Jesus once cried, "Jerusalem, Jerusalem, who kills the prophets and stones those who are sent to her! How often I wanted to gather your children together, the way a hen gathers her chicks under her wings, and you were unwilling" (Matthew 23:37). Can you hear the pain and the longing in His words? All He desires is our salvation, "For the Son of Man has come to seek and to save that which was lost" (Luke 19:10). He was so in love with mankind and was so unwilling for souls to perish that He stepped out of heaven, took on human flesh, and became a substitutionary sacrifice on the cross to receive God's wrath in order to ransom our souls.

This is a true example of a missionary, of an intercessor. It is someone who is willing to leave their own comfort in order to stand in the gap for someone else to come to God even if it means sacrificing themselves in the process. It is through this type of commitment in prayer that souls are won.

Prayer as Warfare for the Souls of Men

We must understand that we are in a spiritual battle for the souls of men. The Bible says that "the god of this world has blinded the minds of the unbelieving so that they might not see the light of the gospel of the glory of Christ, who is the image of God" (2 Corinthians 4:4). The enemy has this world blind and bound. He has no intention of letting go of a single person. He desires to see every human being, young and old, rotting in hell. He tries to kill them before they are even born. Those who are born are then brought into a world full of death, destruction, and despair.

So we must understand that we are not fighting against God, trying to convince Him to save the lost. No. God is already on our side. We are not fighting against God, but "against the rulers, against the powers, against the world forces of this darkness, against the spiritual *forces* of wickedness in the heavenly *places*" (Ephesians 6:12). We are wrestling against Satan and his minions. We are fighting so that Satan's grip would be loosened and his finger pried from the souls of men and women. We are fighting so that people would be able to see through his deception.

It is no wonder many Christians do not pray and do not travail for the souls of men. This is not for the faint of heart. This is not for the cowardly or the comfortable. This is not for those who are living double lives in sin. Leonard Ravenhill says, "The secret of praying is praying in secret. A sinning man will stop praying, and a praying man will stop sinning."[62]

When I came to the Lord in 2004, by the grace of God, I would regularly spend between three and six hours

---

[62] *Why Revival Tarries*, 26.

151

in prayer a day. I can tell you, time in the presence of God is the sweetest thing anyone can experience. I had many supernatural experiences during those times, but what I really gained from those times was an intimate understanding of God's heart. And one thing God would frequently do is burden my heart with the need to pray for souls. I would pray with tears, in agony, sometimes screaming into my pillow so that my family wouldn't hear me.

Although, to be honest, I have many more responsibilities, I still make every effort to spend as many hours with God as I can on a daily basis. And on many occasions when I pray for certain individuals I can literally feel the demonic oppression surrounding their lives. This type of intercessory prayer for souls doesn't work like magic. Many times we must be tenacious and it might take years, but I have chosen not to back down from this fight and will try to win as many people as I can in prayer.

[63]Amy W. Carmichael wrote,

> O for a passionate passion for souls,
>
> O for a pity that yearns!
>
> O for the love that loves unto death,
>
> O for the fire that burns!
>
> O for the pure prayer-power that prevails,
>
> That pours itself out for the lost!
>
> Victorious prayer in the Conquerors Name,

---

[63] Ibid, 108.

O for a PENTECOST!

Making it Practical

You might already be convinced that you would like to pray for souls more but are not sure on how to go about it. Let me give you some practical advice.

1. Choose a place and a time

I remember hearing Charles Stanley saying, "before you learn to pray any-where at any-time you must learn to pray some-where at some-time." In other words, if you want to make a discipline of praying then you must make space for it in your daily schedule. If prayer is a priority for you then you will find a time and a place where you can spend time with God. Pick a time where you are the most alert and will not be too distracted or exhausted. Then choose a place where you can talk to God without a problem.[64] It is important you form a discipline in your prayer time.

2. Take time to read the word and worship God

If you want to pray with God's heart and with His perspective it is important that you spend time in His word, where His will is revealed. Knowing His will, will allow you to pray with authority and conviction. But you also want to worship because in worship God is elevated, in your own mind, above every enemy and circumstance keeping a soul from salvation. As I have heard some say, "it is impossible to worry and worship at the same time." Through worship, you get to encounter and experience God

---

[64] If you would like a good series on prayer please watch the series of Robert Morris or read his book called *Frequency*.

Himself, not just intellectually, but from spirit to spirit. This allows God to impress His heart upon yours. As a result you will not pray out of a sense of duty, but out of a compassion that is flowing from the very heart of God. You will want others to experience His goodness as you do.

3. Have a list of people that you can consistently present to God in prayer

Although we want the whole world to come to Christ, it is easier to set your focus on a few. Because there already is a natural affection for those you know, begin with family and friends that God impresses upon your heart. It will be easier to pray for them than to pray for a complete stranger unless God burdens you with such a person. Make a list of five to ten names that you will commit to praying for regularly until something happens.

4. Declare God's word and come against any opposition

I mentioned earlier that praying for souls is warfare. For that reason you must know what weapons you possess and how to use them if you want to be effective. The Bible says that God's word is actually "the sword of the Spirit" (Ephesians 6:17). So arm yourself with Biblical promises that you can declare over the person(s) you are praying for. Find verses that have to do with salvation, deliverance, healing, and God-encounters. Bind the strongman operating in the person's life (Matthew 12:29). Pray for their spiritual eyes to be opened (Ephesians 1:18). You can even personalize scriptures for them if you don't know what to say, for example "I pray 'Juan' would be filled with the knowledge of Your will in all spiritual wisdom and understanding, so that 'Juan' will walk in a manner worthy of the Lord, to please Him in all respects, bearing fruit in every good work and increasing in the knowledge of God" (Colossians 1:9-10). Or "God, you are not willing that 'Juan' should perish but that he would come to repentance (2 Peter 3:9) so I ask you to convict 'Juan' of sin, righteousness and judgment (John 16:8) so that he would call upon your name and be saved (Romans 10:13).

5. Expect God to work

Maintain your faith throughout the process. Sometimes it may look like the person is getting worse and that your prayers are not having any effect. But remember the promise of God, "The effective prayer of a righteous man can accomplish much" (James 5:16). Your prayers are working and the circumstances and attitude you see may just be them resisting the conviction of the Holy Spirit or God positioning them for a breakthrough. He might allow them to hit rock bottom so that the only direction they can look is up at God. As you invest time in these persons, continue praying for each of them until they surrender or until God lifts the burden for them off of your heart.

So, will you give time to praying for the lost? Will you allow God to burden your heart with souls until the pain is so deep that you cannot even articulate words as you passionately plead for their salvation? We must preach, we must evangelize but we must also pray.

Revival and Evangelism

For this reason it says, 'Awake, sleeper, And arise from the dead, And Christ will shine on you.' (Ephesians 5:14)

The times of the greatest outreach are during the time of revivals. This has been seen throughout the history of the Church and also in the Bible. My heart yearns to see the floods of revival sweep this nation and all the world once again. It is my conviction that the greatest harvest of souls come during periods of revival.

There are many who have written and spoken on this subject of revival. I will not try to compete or attack anyone's particular view. I am not a theologian nor a revival historian. But I would just like to give my humble and limited perspective on this subject based on what I have received from time in prayer and in the Word. Much of what I am going to share is what I believe the Holy Spirit has shown me during long seasons of prayer and reflection on this subject which is so dear to my heart.

What is Revival?

Like a flood breaking through a dam, revival is when the kingdom of God breaks through this realm through a great outpouring of the Holy Spirit. When God pours out His Spirit in this way, the Spirit brings the kingdom and releases it in our midst in a mighty way. Revival is the closest manifestation of the kingdom of God on the earth before Jesus' returns.

I have based this understanding on three examples of revival in the New Testament. I believe revival occurred in Acts 2, 8, and 19.

Examples of Revival in the Book of Acts

In Acts 2, we see the fulfillment of the promise made by the Father in the book of Joel chapter 2. Peter quotes this promise in verses 17 to 21

> [17] And it shall be in the last days, God says, That I will pour forth of My Spirit on all mankind; And your sons and your daughters shall prophesy, And your young men shall see visions, And your old men shall dream dreams; [18] Even on My bondslaves, both men and women, I will in those days pour forth of My Spirit And they shall prophesy. [19] And I will grant wonders in the sky above And signs on the earth below, Blood, and fire, and vapor of smoke. [20] The sun will be turned into darkness And the moon into blood, Before the great and glorious day of the Lord shall come. [21] And it shall be that everyone who calls on the name of the Lord will be saved.

The beginning of the fulfillment of this promise occurred on the day of Pentecost after a time of extended prayer.

> When the day of Pentecost had come, they were all together in one place. [2] And suddenly there came from heaven a noise like a violent rushing wind, and it filled the whole house where they were sitting. [3] And there appeared

> to them tongues as of fire distributing them-
> selves, and they rested on each one of them.
> ⁴ And they were all filled with the Holy Spirit
> and began to speak with other tongues, as the
> Spirit was giving them utterance. (2:1-4)

By the end of the day, 3,000 people had given their life to
Jesus in the city of Jerusalem – the very same city where
He was rejected and crucified (v41).

Then in obedience to Jesus' mandate to be His witnesses in "Jerusalem, and in all Judea, Samaria and even in
the remotest part of the earth" (1:8) the next place we see
something similar is in Samaria. After persecution had broken out in Jerusalem and Judea many Christians had to flee.
But as they fled they began to minister wherever they went.

> ⁴ Therefore, those who had been scattered
> went about preaching the word. ⁵ Philip went
> down to the city of Samaria and *began* pro-
> claiming Christ to them. ⁶ The crowds with
> one accord were giving attention to what was
> said by Philip, as they heard and saw the signs
> which he was performing. ⁷ For *in the case of*
> many who had unclean spirits, they were
> coming out *of them* shouting with a loud
> voice; and many who had been paralyzed and
> lame were healed. ⁸ So there was much rejoic-
> ing in that city. (8:4-8)

The revival in that city was so mighty that even the most
powerful magician, Simon, who had deceived the whole
city with his magic arts (8:9-11) believed the gospel and got
baptized (v13).

And lastly, we see in chapter 19 that Paul goes to the city of Ephesus. And as he stayed a few years teaching about the kingdom of God in the synagogues, he was also preaching and performing great signs among the people of the city. "[11] God was performing extraordinary miracles by the hands of Paul, [12] so that handkerchiefs or aprons were even carried from his body to the sick, and the diseases left them and the evil spirits went out" (19:11-12).

As a result of what God was doing through Paul,

> "[18] Many also of those who had believed kept coming, confessing and disclosing their practices. [19] And many of those who practiced magic brought their books together and *began* burning them in the sight of everyone; and they counted up the price of them and found it fifty thousand pieces of silver. [20] So the word of the Lord was growing mightily and prevailing." (v18-20)

The Signs of Revival

After studying these three passages where I noticed revival taking place I observed eight elements that can be described as signs of a revival.[65] These eight elements, qualities, or occurrences can be seen in most revivals throughout church history.

1. The church is brought back to her first love

---

[65] I added points 2 and 8 after further reflection and reading of other material. It is also important to note that not every revival will manifest all eight points. But certain elements will almost always show up like the conviction of sin and holy living or the conversion of multitudes of sinners.

If you notice, the very same disciples who had once been discouraged and afraid after the death of Jesus had received new life and passion after seeing Him rise from the dead and then receiving this outpouring of the Holy Spirit. They returned to their first love.

There are many churches and Christians today that are without joy or zeal. They are religious, focused on outward appearances, formalities and traditions of men. They are without power, Biblically illiterate and spiritually lazy. They may be doing many of the right things, but they have lost their first love.[66]

But when revival comes, the church is brought back to that first love. Some good synonyms for first love are hunger, and holy dissatisfaction and desperation. A Christian who is in his first love is like a hungry man. He seeks, feeds, and nourishes himself with the presence of God. A Christian in his first love maintains a holy dissatisfaction. Nothing can satisfy him but being in the presence of God. There is a desperation in how he seeks His Lord. He spends as many moments as possible reading His word, persevering in prayer, serving His people, loving and exhorting sinners with the gospel. His eyes are focused. His mind is narrow. He only see's one thing, wants one thing, desires one thing – to remain in the love and presence of God. His highest pleasure is obeying God. Holiness for him is not a burden but a privilege.

2. There is a deep conviction of sin and holy living

J. Edwin Orr, a revival historian, said, "Revival is like judgement day." What he meant by that is that when

---

[66] See Revelation 2:1-7

the Holy Spirit is poured out He brings strong impressions of conviction. Jesus told us that when the Holy Spirit would come He would "convict the world of sin, righteousness and judgment" (John 16:8). And so the hideousness of sin is magnified in the presence of the Holy one. With such a tangibility of the presence of the Holy Spirit, people will begin to confess and repent of deep hidden sins. People have even been reported to faint under the weight of such conviction during times of revival.

But afterwards, waves of forgiveness rush over the people and there is much peace and rejoicing as people gain an understanding that God has washed away their sins in the blood of Jesus. This then propels the people into new levels of consecration and holy living. Larger percentages of people remain faithful and do not backslide when converted or consecrated during times of revival.

3. The Great Commission is fulfilled with new passion and fire

When Christians return to their first love and consecrate their lives they are filled with new fire and desire to talk about the person they are in love with – Jesus. It is no longer just a discipline for them. Now they can't help but go around and speak about Jesus. They are so excited and full of joy to spread the gospel. This becomes contagious and people begin to respond. Believer's hearts begin to over flow and they are willing to go to the end of the world even to reach one person and share the good news of salvation. Notice that in each of these revivals preaching spread like wildfire.

4. Sinners are converted in great quantities

With all these Christians speaking about Jesus and the abundant presence of the Holy Spirit empowering their words many sinners begin to listen and turn to God. They begin to come under conviction. It is said that even during the Welsh Revival of the early 1900's that bars and clubs began to close, crime began to decrease. Some people would even convert without any one preaching to them. The presence of God was so thick over the city. In Jerusalem, first 3,000 and then 5,000 (Acts 4:4), and then the cities of Samaria and Ephesus saw great numbers of sinners turning to Jesus!

Here are some passages that speak of the great increase in the book of Acts. "And all the more believers in the Lord, multitudes of men and women, were constantly added to *their number*" (5:14). "The word of God kept on spreading; and the number of the disciples continued to increase greatly in Jerusalem, and a great many of the priests were becoming obedient to the faith" (6:7). "So the church throughout all Judea and Galilee and Samaria enjoyed peace, being built up; and going on in the fear of the Lord and in the comfort of the Holy Spirit, it continued to increase" (9:31). "And the hand of the Lord was with them, and a large number who believed turned to the Lord" (11:21). "And considerable numbers were brought to the Lord" (11:24). "But the word of the Lord continued to grow and to be multiplied" (12:24). "So the churches were being strengthened in the faith, and were increasing in number daily" (16:5).[67]

5. Supernatural signs and wonders break out

---

[67] Geoff Waugh, *Revival Fires: History's Mighty Revivals* (Mechanicsburg, PA: The Apostolic Network of Global Awakening, 2011), 17.

Wherever revival goes miracles follow. Remember revival is about the Holy Spirit bringing the kingdom and so the supernatural begins to follow believers and confirm their message. We can see miracles, healings and deliverances abound as the grace of God overwhelms the people.

6. Societal structures are impacted and changed by Biblical principles

With the conversion of so many sinners things begin to change within the very heart and culture of a city. In Ephesus the people were burning up their books and paraphernalia of witchcraft. They stopped buying idols from the merchants. If you change a heart, you can change a life. If you change a life, you can change a family. If you change a family, you can change a neighborhood. If you can change a neighborhood, you can change a city. If you can change a city, you can change a nation. If you can change a nation, you can change the world!

Just imagine the crime and immorality in your neighborhood going down. Just imagine the poor and people with addictions being helped and delivered. Just imagine a city full of love, the gospel, and justice. This can happen! It happens during times of revival!

7. The kingdom and works of Satan are uprooted and destroyed

When revival comes, the blindfolds on people's eyes begin to fall off; the strongholds in their minds begin to crumble; their sinful addictions begin to be destroyed. People begin to be delivered from spirits of depression, PTSD, schizophrenia, lust, and bitterness. The witches and sorcerers begin to lose their power over the people.

8. Unity in the Body of Christ

Although unity can be a precursor to revival it is also a result of revival. Look at what Acts 2:42-46 says,

> They were continually devoting themselves to the apostles' teaching and to fellowship, to the breaking of bread and to prayer. [43] Everyone kept feeling a sense of awe; and many wonders and signs were taking place through the apostles. [44] And all those who had believed were together and had all things in common; [45] and they *began* selling their property and possessions and were sharing them with all, as anyone might have need. [46] Day by day continuing with one mind in the temple, and breaking bread from house to house, they were taking their meals together with gladness and sincerity of heart.

When revival comes color lines are washed away by the blood.[68] Doctrinal distinctions, though important, become secondary to the "unity of the Spirit" (Ephesians 4:3) and what people have in common in Christ. This is the desire of Christ's heart, "that they may all be one; even as You, Father, *are* in Me and I in You, that they also may be in Us, so that the world may believe that You sent Me" (John 17:21).[69]

---

[68] Waugh, 91.

[69] Even though this is so, this does not mean that everyone is always on the same page. Persecution could be added to the list of what happens during revival. Opposition always arises from without and from within the body of Christ. People slander what they do not understand and sometimes prefer

I am telling you we need revival, and we need it now!

How does Revival Come?

This question can be very controversial. The question that is debated in many theological circles is, "Is revival something that God sends sovereignly in His time or can man provoke God to send a revival whenever man wants? In other words, does revival come only when God wants or can man provoke God to send revival at any time?

I believe the answer is YES! God will send revival only when He wants and at the same time He can be provoked whenever we desire revival.

Here are some questions we must ask ourselves: According to our definition of revival, is it His will to pour out His Spirit mightily? Is it His will for His kingdom to come, for His will to be done here on earth as it is in heaven? Is it God's will for the church to live in its first love? For sinners to be converted? For the works of Satan to be destroyed?

I think we would all nod our head, yes. So the next question we need to ask ourselves is, is it God's will for this all to happen today? If it is, then why don't we have a revival right now? Why are we not experiencing revival right now?

I am in agreement with Leonard Ravenhill. The greatest reason we do not have revival now is because we

---

to hold on to their traditions and their positions. Sometimes even gross imitations and distortions will arise and be used against genuine revivals. The best way to know if what the opposition is saying is true is by investigating for yourself, and not just taking someone else's word on it. If possible show up and form your own conclusions.

don't really want it. We are not willing to pay the price. I believe it is God's will for us to have revival, and to have it right now. But in order to experience revival we must be willing to pay the price.

To see revival I believe we need to be willing to, number one, humble ourselves before God. 2 Chronicles 7:14 says, if "My people who are called by My name humble themselves and pray and seek My face and turn from their wicked ways, then I will hear from heaven, will forgive their sin and will heal their land." The Bible says that God gives grace to the humble, but He will oppose the proud (James 4:6).

Number two, we must be willing to pray tenaciously until it comes. To pray tenaciously means to pray persistently, firmly, constantly, consistently, and perseveringly. The Bible says, "Pray without ceasing" (1 Thessalonians 5:17). The Bible says, "Devote yourselves to prayer" (Colossians 4:2). Jesus taught us to keep on asking, keep on seeking and keep on knocking (Matthew 7:7).

Did you know that the Moravians, in 1727, made a covenant to pray around the clock, 24 hours a day to fulfill Leviticus 6:13, "Fire shall be kept burning continually on the altar; it is not to go out." They did this for the purpose of missions and this prayer covenant lasted for 100 years! As a result of this incessant prayer they started a powerful missionary movement and even impacted the life of John Wesley who was a great leader in the First Great Awakening.

Number three, we must seek to be filled with the Holy Spirit. Lastly, we must go out in obedience to fulfill the Great Commission.

It is when these conditions are fulfilled that we can expect to see revival come to our churches, streets, communities, and cities. Here is something I wrote in my journal October 31, 2016.

I believe a revival is coming to this city. And this revival will be known as the Love Revival. It will be a revival of love. There will be healing, miracles, deliverances, and great evangelism, but it will all be rooted in love, motivated by love, and seen as a movement of love. We will share Jesus, serve others, pray for others, and win souls not just because it is the right thing to do; not just because we must and have been commanded to. No. We will do it because we won't be able to help ourselves. We won't be able to *not* share Jesus, help and serve others, or pray for others because our hearts will be so full of love that it will spill over into the streets, into the homes, into our workplace, into our schools, into our families and into our city. We won't be able to help but love people. We will see people through God's eyes. We will have a heavenly vision. We will not be discouraged because of sin, intimidated by evil, or hindered by injustice because we will see everything and everyone from God's eyes, from eyes of love. God will be bigger to us than their failures, their sin, their wrongs, and their hardness. We will be loving bulldozers. People will come from all around and this Love Revival will infect cities, nations, churches and movements. What glory will come! What glory we will see!

I see a Bronx filled with love and the power of God. I see a city that will seek justice and peace. I declare this city will no longer be known for its great sin, its rap music or its violence.

I hope you would be stirred to pray for revival to come to your city, your nation or your neighborhood. But before it goes across the world, revival must come to you first. Will you join me in seeking this revival? I know it is God's will. I know I will see it in my time and I want to be a part of it. Do you?

Conclusion

This book is the second in my series "ChristLike." My heart's desire is that we would live up to our names as "Christians." That we would demonstrate that we are followers of Jesus in every area of our lives. That we would want to imitate everything about Him, including how He evangelized.

Maybe, after everything you've read you disagree with my perspective on evangelism. That's ok. But allow me to ask you some questions: How would you define evangelism? Would your definition fit with the example and life of Jesus and the New Testament church? How did Jesus and His followers evangelize?

Whatever your answers are to those questions is what you should be practicing and demonstrating. What I know is that when I look at the teaching and the lives of Jesus and the Early Church leaders I see that evangelism, to them, involved both the sharing of a message and a demonstration of God's power. In relation to sharing the gospel Randy Clark says:

> The issue, then, is when we hear the word *gospel* today, do we tend to hear it through the voices of sixteenth-century reformers, whose focus was on salvation, rather than from the voices of the first-century missionaries, apostles, church planters, evangelists, healers, prophets, pastors, and teachers who saw the gospel more as *Christus Victor* – be-

cause of Jesus' death on the cross, His resurrection from the dead, and His ascension, He has won the victory over the strongman, the devil. As a result of this victory, in His name, not only is there forgiveness of sin and reconciliation to God resulting in eternal life, but there is also power over disease, demons, the devil, and damnation. Healing and miracles are part and parcel of the good news of the Kingdom. They are not primarily to confirm the message, but are to be an expression of the message, a part of the message.[70]

If we want to fish for men like Jesus did we need to follow both His example and His instructions. "And He sent them out to proclaim the kingdom of God and to perform healing" (Luke 9:2). We must preach the gospel, the good news of who Jesus is and what He has done for us. And we must also demonstrate it with signs following.

Be salt and light. Give to the poor, take care of the widow and the orphan, visit the sick, reach out to your communities in any way you can. But don't forget to evangelize with power and you will see a great harvest come to Jesus. "Truly, truly, I say to you, he who believes in Me, the works that I do, he will do also; and greater *works* than these he will do; because I go to the Father" (John 14:12).

And He said to them, "Go into all the world and preach the gospel to all creation. [16] He who has believed and has been baptized shall be saved; but he who has disbelieved shall be condemned. [17] These signs will accompany

---

[70] *Authority to Heal* (Shippensburg, PA: Destiny Image, 2016), 135.

those who have believed: in My name they will cast out demons, they will speak with new tongues; [18] they will pick up serpents, and if they drink any deadly *poison*, it will not hurt them; they will lay hands on the sick, and they will recover."

[19] So then, when the Lord Jesus had spoken to them, He was received up into heaven and sat down at the right hand of God. [20] And they went out and preached everywhere, while the Lord worked with them, and confirmed the word by the signs that followed. (Mark 16:15-20)

Pursue love, for without it everything we do is meaningless. Preach the gospel, for it is the power of God for salvation. Be filled with the Holy Spirit, for when you are you will be clothed with power and will be witnesses for Christ in your Jerusalem, your Judea, your Samaria, and to the ends of the earth.

Appendix: Treasure Hunt

I would like to recommend a form of evangelism that will utilize everything that you have learned about in this book. This form of evangelism is fun yet challenging, practical yet effective, and depends completely on the supernatural from beginning to end. This is something that you can do alone or in a group, which is actually better. It is called a Treasure Hunt.

Kevin Dedmon, in his book *The Ultimate Treasure Hunt*, describes a way of reaching souls through super- natural encounters and revelation. Dedmon relates that we are God's treasure and just as Jesus left everything to seek us and save us, we can join God in "hunting for treasures" so that they may know Him. The process of tracking down treasures is partly based on the story found in Acts 9 when God speaks to Ananias about Saul of Tarsus. He gives him supernatural instructions through words of knowledge to go to a particular street, find a particular home, meet a particular person, and pray for a particular need (9:10-19).

Everywhere around us there are sinners, but the treasure hunts help us to target those people who might be more open to receiving and hearing from God. From this story Dedmon has developed a strategy on how to find souls that are in need of a word or touch from God. And so the way this works is that a person should try to do this in a group of 3 to 4 people maximum. This group of treasure hunters should then spend a moment in prayer and petition God to reveal to them someone He wants them to reach with His love.

After a brief moment in prayer everyone should be ready to fill out their own individual "treasure map" with the words of knowledge they received when in prayer. The treasure map is a list that will be compiled of the details received from God. The things you will look to write down are: location, person's name, person's appearance, person's need, and anything unusual. You should not write down paragraphs of information, just brief descriptions and words.

Location: What is God showing you of where the person might be? (stop sign, bench, digital clock, coffee shop, Target, Wal-Mart, etc.)

Person's name: What name or names did God put in your heart for that person? (John, Mary, etc.)

Person's appearance: What might the person be wearing or what do they look like? (the color of their specific articles of clothing, the color of their hair, etc.)

Person's need: What might they need prayer for? (knee brace, cane, kidneys, tumor, left ankle, marriage, etc.)

Anything unusual: What came to mind that doesn't fit the other categories or that you are not sure of what God meant? (lollipop, windmill, lime-green door, dolphins, etc.)[71]

On one occasion last year, after I had taught the youth how to do this, they decided to try it out. They got together and broke up into smaller groups. On their very first try, after combining the details in each other's maps

---

[71] Adapted from the appendix in *The Ultimate Treasure Hunt* by Kevin Dedmon.

they were able to minister to someone who matched the descriptions they had written. For example, one person had "black shades," another had "white shirt," another had "depression," and another one had "braids." When they went out treasure hunting, after some time walking they found a female, with braided hair, wearing a white V-neck shirt and black shades hanging from her shirt. They approached her and explained what they were doing. Then they asked her if she was dealing with depression. The woman immediately began to cry. She confessed to them that she was dealing with severe depression and was even contemplating suicide. They ended up praying for her and ministering to that need!

They had a successful treasure hunt. I on the other hand, on my first attempt, failed miserably. First, the people I did it with had their own ideas of how the treasure hunt was supposed to work. And second, the details we had written down didn't come to pass. Some were too general. For instance, I had "black hair and black coat" for appearance. It was winter when this happened. Most of the people outside had black hair and black coats! I stopped at least 3 people with that description and none of them had any of the other details on any of our lists! We did get to pray for someone who had a need that was on our lists and had a black coat and black hair. But it wasn't spot on.

I say this, first of all, to let you know that not everyone will have a successful experience every time. Do not get discouraged. Second, I would suggest that whoever you team up with understands the concept of the treasure hunt and that everyone is in one mind and heart about what is going to happen. Third, you do not have to be "super spiritual" to do this. Kids can do this. Recent converts can do this. So do not over-think this. Just write down whatever images, thoughts or impressions you receive when in prayer. Even if you are not sure, write it down. Fourth, use each other's maps to combine details. For example, your list might have a person's name, while someone else has the physical appearance, and another person has the need, etc. Each list, by itself, does not contain all the details for the person. This will be a team effort. Of course, this will not be the case if you choose to do it alone. Lastly, just have fun. You are doing this out of love and because you have something from God to share. So do not be afraid, step out in faith.

This is just a brief overview. If you want to know more about doing treasure hunts buy his books on this topic and then put it into practice. This is a great way to build your faith and reliance on the Holy Spirit. Every gift will be utilized in this exercise. It's a great way to train and encourage yourself and others to step out in faith and evangelize with the supernatural power of God. So step out in faith and follow in the steps of Jesus and the disciples of the early church. Power evangelism is Christ-like evangelism.

Bibliography

Baker Publishing Group. 2004. "Power Through Prayer." In *The Complete Works of E. M. Bounds on Prayer*, by E. M. Bounds, 445-493. Grand Rapids, MI: Baker Books.

Bosworth, F. F. 2008. *Christ the Healer.* Grand Rapids, MI: Chosen Books.

Brooks, Steven. 2014. *How to Operate in the Gifts of the Spirit.* Shippensburg, PA: Destiny Image.

Clark, Randy and Timothy Berry and Annie Byrne and Chris Ishak. 2011. *Entertaining Angels: Engaging the Unseen Realm.* Mechanicsburg, PA: Apostolic Network of Global Awakening.

Clark, Randy. 2016. *Authority to Heal.* Shippensburg, PA: Destiny Image.

—. 2015. *The Biblical Guidebook to Deliverance.* Lake Mary, Fl: Charisma House. Kindle Edition.

—. 2011. *Words of Knowledge.* Mechanicsburg, PA: Apostolic Network of Global Awakening. Kindle Edition.

Dedmon, Kevin. 2007. *The Ultimate Treasure Hunt.* Shippensburg, PA: Destiny Image.

Medic, Praying. 2015. *Divine Healing Made Simple.* Gilbert, AZ: Inkity Press TM. Kindle Edition.

Ravenhill, Leonard. 1987. *Why Revival Tarries.* Minneapolis, MN: Bethany House.

Stanley, Charles. n.d. *In Touch Daily Devotions.* http://www.intouch.org/read/magazine/daily-devotions/how-to-increase-your-faith.

Thomas, Art. 2011. *The Word of Knowledge in Action.* Shippensburg, PA: Destiny Image. Kindle Edition.

—."10 Things Jesus Never Said About Healing". YouTube video, 1:10:21. Posted February 2014. https://www.youtube.com/watch?v=hHDKIfcbn2g.

Valloton, Kris. 2014. *Basic Training for the Prophetic Ministry.* Shippensburg, PA: Destiny Image. Kindle Edition.

Waugh, Geoff. 2011. *Revival Fires: History's Mighty Revivals.* Mechanicsburg, PA: The Apostolic Network of Global Awakening.

Recommended Material

Besides what is listed in the Bibliography, the following are some good materials to help you continue growing in and increasing your hunger for the supernatural.

Videos by Art Thomas, Todd White, Dan Mohler, Randy Clark, Bill Johnson, and Sid Roth on YouTube

God's Generals series by Roberts Liardon

There is More, The Essential Guide to the Power of the Holy Spirit and *Power to Heal* by Randy Clark

Pain in Full by Art Thomas

Authentic Fire by Michael L. Brown

Victory Over the Darkness, *The Bondage Breaker* by Neil T. Anderson

4 Keys to Hearing God's Voice by Mark Virkler

Prophetic Evangelism Made Simple by Matthew Robert Payne

Power Evangelism by John Wimber

Hearing God's Voice and *Seeing in the Spirit* by Praying Medic

Lectures on Revivals of Religion by Charles G. Finney

The Awakening by Friedrich Zundel

Azusa Street by Frank Bartleman

Translating God by Shawn Bolz

Dreams and Visions by Jane Hamon

They Shall Expel Demons by Derek Prince

Supernatural Forces in Spiritual Warfare by Peter Wagner

2000 Years of Charismatic Christianity by Eddie L. Hyatt

School of the Prophets by Kris Valloton

The Fourth Dimension by Dr. David Yonggi Cho

The Jesus Fast by Lou Engle and Dean Briggs

Listen to Me Satan! by Carlos Annacondia

Spiritual Gifts and Their Operations by Howard Carter

The first book of this series, *ChristLike: Following in His Footsteps*, is available for free as a PDF. Request a copy by emailing schjjv@msn.com.

* 9 7 8 0 9 9 9 1 2 5 4 0 3 *